More Praise for *How to Be a Positive*

"Profound, practical, inspirational. Writte[n]
ers in positive organizational scholarsh[ip]
based recommendations provide a con[ ]
application. This is a must-read for leaders who wish to broaden and ___ on
the positive impact they can have on organizations."
—**Jim Loehr, cofounder and Vice President, Human Performance Institute**

"We need many more positive leaders in our society and in business. Positive
leaders create possibility for others. They help us do the right thing and enable
us to lead more extraordinary lives. This book is filled with practical advice
about how you can become a positive leader. Bravo!"
—**R. Edward Freeman, University Professor, Darden School of Business,**
  University of Virginia

"This insightful and actionable book beautifully articulates a very relevant and
timely set of positive leadership principles. The arrangement of the tools in
'bite-size' segments is the perfect format for any leader to present."
—**Fred Keller, Chairman and CEO, Cascade Engineering**

"Every chapter I read struck a chord and made me rethink an element of my own
leadership. This book beautifully combines inspirational ideas with high quality
evidence. It is thoughtful, insightful, and brimming with fresh approaches."
—**Sharon Parker, Winthrop Professor, UWA Business School, University of**
  Western Australia

"Thirteen insightful essays and about 800 good ideas one can implement for
immediate improvement. You'd have to be wildly negative in your worldview
not to walk away from reading this book with a wealth of tangible, doable action steps to take your leadership and your organization's work performance
to the next level."
—**Ari Weinzweig, Cofounding Partner, Zingerman's Community of Businesses**

"Every leader and aspiring leader from all sectors of society should enjoy, learn,
and be inspired by this practical and highly engaging new volume. Don't miss
this opportunity to learn how to dramatically improve your leadership skills and
make a larger positive impact throughout your career."
—**Stewart I. Donaldson, Dean and Professor of Psychology, Claremont Graduate**
  University

"The Center for Positive Organizations is a treasure trove of people and knowledge. Now we have the map to their treasure. *How to Be a Positive Leader*
gives us a practical path to become better, positive, inspirational leaders."
—**Rich Sheridan, CEO, Menlo Innovations LLC**

"Jane Dutton and Gretchen Spreitzer have gathered a sterling group of thought leaders to describe what it takes to become a positive leader. Thought-provoking and provocative, it shows the day-to-day actions leaders can take right now to improve the quality of relationships, build the capacity for collaboration, and unlock the resources of innovation. A must-read for any practicing leader or those destined to follow the extraordinary trajectory to positive leadership."
—**Lynda Gratton, Professor of Management Practice, London Business School**

"Jane Dutton and Gretchen Spreitzer have tapped the greatest minds to provide a one-stop resource for leaders who want to create and maintain a meaningful, purposeful, and positive workplace. The leadership tools and experiences discussed play to the desires of leaders to inspire themselves and others; promote excellence, virtuousness, and high quality connections; and reward positive deviance in the workplace to bring about exponential positive change."
—**Roger Newton, founder, Executive Chairman, and Chief Scientific Officer, Esperion Therapeutics, Inc.**

"As Gallup polls proclaim that seven in ten American workers are disengaged, this book provides a recipe for change. Simultaneously theoretically rigorous and action oriented, the authors offer concrete actions to recreate yourself and spur others to thrive. As leaders seek to move their organizations to higher levels of excellence, this book provides simple but powerful tools to improve relationships and excitement about the future."
—**Deborah Ancona, Seley Distinguished Professor of Management and Faculty Director, MIT Leadership Center, MIT Sloan School of Management**

"The book offers distilled and accessible wisdom from many years of solid research. It is a tour de force of positive leadership, written with a deep sense of humanity and providing a plethora of concrete practices to make an impact."
—**Arne Carlsen, Associate Professor, BI Norwegian Business School**

"'What do I *do*?' That's the biggest question we hear from leaders who want to create positive organizations. This book is the answer. It gives you specific actions, inspiring examples, and even tweets. Apply this book and you will be a positive leader."
—**Wayne Baker, Professor of Management and Organizations, University of Michigan, and author of *United America***

"Positive organization studies is a burgeoning field of evidence-based management that, enacted in everyday organizational life, makes a real difference. Organizational dysfunctions need remedies, and many can be found in the wisdom assembled in these chapters."
—**Stewart Clegg, Professor, University of Technology, Sydney**

HOW TO BE A
POSITIVE LEADER

HOW TO BE A
POSITIVE LEADER

SMALL ACTIONS, BIG IMPACT

JANE E. DUTTON and
GRETCHEN M. SPREITZER

Berrett–Koehler Publishers, Inc.
San Francisco
a BK Business book

Berrett-Koehler Publishers, Inc.
235 Montgomery Street, Suite 650
San Francisco, CA 94104-2916
Tel: (415) 288-0260   Fax: (415) 362-2512
www.bkconnection.com

Ordering Information

QUANTITY SALES. Special discounts are available on quantity purchases by corporations,
associations, and others. For details, contact the "Special Sales Department" at the
Berrett-Koehler address above.

INDIVIDUAL SALES. Berrett-Koehler publications are available through most bookstores.
They can also be ordered directly from Berrett-Koehler: Tel: (800) 929-2929; Fax: (802) 864-7626;
www.bkconnection.com

ORDERS FOR COLLEGE TEXTBOOK/COURSE ADOPTION USE. Please contact
Berrett-Koehler: Tel: (800) 929-2929; Fax: (802) 864-7626.
Orders by U.S. trade bookstores and wholesalers. Please contact Ingram Publisher Services,
Tel: (800) 509-4887; Fax: (800) 838-1149; E-mail: customer.service@ingrampublisherservices.com;
or visit www.ingrampublisherservices.com/Ordering for details about electronic ordering.

Berrett-Koehler and the BK logo are registered trademarks of Berrett-Koehler Publishers, Inc.
Printed in the United States of America.

Berrett-Koehler books are printed on long-lasting acid-free paper. When it is available, we
choose paper that has been manufactured by environmentally responsible processes. These
may include using trees grown in sustainable forests, incorporating recycled paper,
minimizing chlorine in bleaching, or recycling the energy produced at the paper mill.

Library of Congress Cataloging-in-Publication Data

How to be a positive leader : small actions, big impact / [edited by] Jane E Dutton and
Gretchen Spreitzer ; foreword by Shawn Achor.
       pages cm
Summary: "The field of positive leadership continues to expand. Building on the practical
tools and philosophy in Kim Cameron's books (including Positive Leadership, over 30,000
copies sold), this edited volume brings the best research from fourteen scholars and translates
it into plain English for organizations"—Provided by publisher.
    ISBN 978-1-62656-028-4 (paperback)
    1. Leadership. 2. Organizational effectiveness—Management. I. Dutton, Jane E. II. Spreitzer,
Gretchen M.
    HD57.7.H683 2014
    658.4'092—dc23
                                                                                    2014005602

First Edition
18 17 16 15 14   10 9 8 7 6 5 4 3 2 1

Cover/Jacket Designer: Leslie Waltzer, Crowfoot Design
Photographer/Artist: Jeffery Coolidge/Getty Images
Interior Design: George Whipple

*To leaders past, present, and future
who call forth the best in people
and in work organizations.*

Contents

Foreword

Shawn Achor

author of *The Happiness Advantage*
and *Before Happiness*

In one of my earliest attempts to bring leadership research into companies, I was invited to Zurich by a large Swiss bank during the economic crisis to give a lecture on Positive Leadership in Uncertain Times. Instead of reading my short bio, a disgruntled senior leader, who had been forced by the Human Resources (HR) Department to introduce my session, came to the front of the room and said, "Hello. As you know, we don't have bonuses for everyone, but here is a talk on happiness . . . from a guy from America."

You can imagine the response. There was immediate non-verbal stonewalling from these cool, reserved Swiss bankers. Honestly, I was already nervous for this talk. I was a green, thirty-year-old researcher with massive educational debts about to lecture on leadership to ultra-wealthy, battle-hardened, fifty-year-old managing directors at one of the world's largest banks. But what happened next was a significant learning moment for me.

About ten minutes into the talk, as I transitioned to explaining the scientific research that had been done on how to create rational optimism and to deepen social support in the midst of crisis, the senior leaders imperceptibly began leaning forward.

Slowly, many began quietly picking up pens and inconspicuously looking for notepads. By the break, ninety minutes into the session, I could not even get to the coffee machine to try one of their fancy espressos because the leaders were flooding me with questions about research that could apply to their team's specific problems. When I finished the three-hour session, I was told by the global head of HR that I would be visiting all of their banking centers in Asia, Europe, and the United States during the banking crisis.

What happened? This book is what happened. The engaged response in Zurich was not about me, it was about the power of positive organizational scholarship. Those Swiss bankers were willing to listen because they respected the rigor with which those researched findings were sought, and they could see the leadership value of those conclusions. Scientifically validated research and focused study of thriving leaders and organizations are the keys to opening minds to real and quantifiable positive change. Without them, we are left with vague motivational statements and a risky reliance on faith in the lecturer rather than in the concepts.

If we want to change the way that organizations work, we need to learn deeply, embrace fully, and communicate effectively this positive research.

Research, of course, is not without error; it is intentionally organic, responding to new findings and rejecting mistaken ones. You will see in this book that these brilliant scholars wrestle with the ideas of their predecessors and contemporaries. But with research comes the ability to extend beyond a single person's ideas to an entire latticework of intrepid scholars seeking to cancel the noise and to find the signal.

It is my belief that there are two major impediments to change. Either we do not know how to change, or we do not believe change is possible. In this book, we attempt to remove these obstacles by helping individuals overcome both mental and physical barriers to change.

Warning: this is not a normal book. Most books do not need instructions; this one does. Most books neatly lay out one or two ideas, all with the same style and structure, and then pound it home. This book is different. The academic scholars who have contributed to this book hail from various universities throughout the nation, and they focus on their own individual topics. If the goal is to get the best information all at once, in truth, no one person could write this book. The collected nature of this book allows you to go directly to the sources of the research to learn how best to use the findings. Perhaps this approach is comparable to the difference between eating boiled, buttered vegetables—where some of the nutrition is cooked out to make it easy to swallow—and eating raw vegetables. This book is more raw than the average reader might be used to, but perhaps the ideas have a greater potential to create positive change.

So I would suggest reading this book as if you were going through an incredible semester of classes taught by rock-star professors. Note well that they all have different styles, just like your favorite professors did in college. Remember that in some classes, you needed to take diligent notes. In others, you needed to scan quickly for the answers you knew would be asked later. In some, you just need to let the information flow over you and hope to absorb genius by osmosis. The key is to take what you can and to apply it immediately. This research is useless unless it is lived. Do not let this book languish on your shelf. Pull the things you need from this text and champion its overarching conclusions: *your behavior matters, and the more positively you lead, the more successful and happy your organization, family, and community will become.*

I am excited by this book, as you can probably tell; these scholars are at the vanguard of their field. Just think about a leader you know at an organization right now who is faced with a challenge. Maybe they want to know how to respond positively to a disengaged team at a call center, or how to help a hospital deal with changes to regulations, or how to over-come culture chasms between two newly merged airlines. It would be incredible for that person to have an entire brain trust of whip-smart individuals who would spend every wak-ing hour for a decade thinking, discussing, writing, and re-searching about that very question. You are holding that brain trust. And after reading and digesting this book fully, you will become that brain trust for your organization. For you are what you read.

Since that learning moment in Zurich, I have had the privi-lege of lecturing in fifty countries and at over a third of the Fortune 100, and I have noticed something interesting. Every company explains to me how they are going through unheard-of change, stress, and workload that differentiates them from every other company or industry. The uniqueness of their situ-ation cannot be the case. And change, stress, and workload are integral parts of work in the modern world; we should not be surprised to find them there.

What I believe *is* different is this: we have reached a unique time where we can no longer increase working hours and work-loads expecting to maximize productivity. We have tripped over the top of the time-management curve and now find the old way of leading, that is, "work harder, longer, and faster," is causing us to work slower, shorter, and more unhappily. We are seeing some of the greatest rates of job dissatisfaction in the history of polling, and younger generations are demanding a change. By immersing yourself in the research in this book, you can help your organization to navigate to a different place by using a different leadership formula. As I wrote in *Before Happiness*, "the greatest competitive advantage in the modern economy is a positive and engaged brain." This book is the research basis for how we can get our brains and organizations to move toward both "positive" and "engaged."

Many of the things that fill the pages of this book could be derived from common sense. But common sense is not common action. Companies and leaders that heed this information will be leading flourishing businesses of the future. A tectonic plate shift is occurring in the nature of how we conceive of work, and those that attempt to reinvent the wheel or do business as usual without a focused, research-based approach to leadership will suffer the fate of the quite fearsome but also quite extinct *T. rex*.

In conclusion, we need you. You are the final ingredient. We need more people finding ways to make this research come alive and to take it beyond the walls of academia into a world that could desperately use it. Information alone will not cause transformation. Sometimes in life, we just do things and they manage to work out. But if you want to truly sustain positive change, you have to understand how to create it well enough to replicate it and to teach it to others.

We hope this book fuels you as you bring this research to life.

Invitation

*Jane E. Dutton and
Gretchen M. Spreitzer*

Some leaders have developed a special set of capabilities, captured in their ability to see possibilities for greatness in people and their team. Other leaders know that small actions can have tremendous impact. We have become believers in both abilities: the power of seeing possibilities and the awareness that small actions can have great impacts for bringing out the best in people and their organizations.

We did not come to this conclusion easily. We have struggled together with our students of all ages as they experience the limits of applying traditional models of leadership in their own lives. Most of us live in systems with scarce resources, where we increasingly must do more with less. Sometimes we lack courage and settle for results that are just "good enough." Over time, fueled by the hope for something more—some oxygen for action—we started exploring new pathways for seeing how leaders could make a difference. We became inspired to write this book to collect and to apply some of the best wisdom available on bringing out the best in people and work organizations. If your job affords opportunities to bring out the best in people at work, then this book is for you. Even if your job does not directly afford you these opportunities, but you care deeply about this goal, this book is for you. Although grounded in strong scholarship and the latest research, we've written this book for you, the leader, not for the researcher.

We have witnessed firsthand the changes made possible when leaders see, know, and act in ways that bring out the best in people and organizations. During the past decade, we have built the Center for Positive Organizations, devoted to understanding how small changes in leaders' actions, particularly if part of "normal practice" in organizations, can be a powerful path toward sustained excellence. Important indicators that an organization and people within it are on this path include meaningful and measurable changes toward increasing greatness. These indicators may be greater task and financial performance, increased thriving and engagement at work, more creativity, greater resilience, and greater overall well-being of individuals and the organization.

A positive leader expects that capacities for excellence can always be expanded. In graphical terms, a positive leader believes in enlarging the zone of possibility for excellence, where today's small actions can change the amount of capacity for excellence inherent in a person or collective over time (see Figure 1). As the figure suggests, "normal" leaders work along the normal path of improving their own or their organization's capacity for excellence. A positive leader believes it is possible to shift the rate and level at which one's own or the organization's capacity for excellence can improve, moving from a normal improvement rate to a more extraordinary improvement rate. The perspectives shared in this book can lift up and accelerate the rate of improvement, increasing the capacity for excellence in significant ways. Expanding the zone of possibility requires new ways of thinking and acting, which are at the heart of positive leadership. *How to Be a Positive Leader* offers a

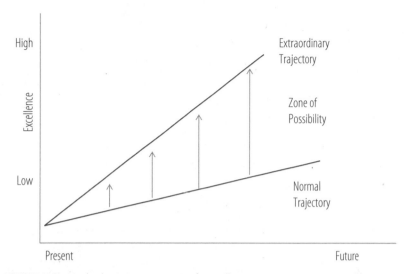

FIGURE 1 Positive leaders increase capacities for excellence.

compelling set of evidence-based perspectives and practices that leaders can embrace, expanding the possibilities for excellence by tapping into the best in people and organizations.

Three features of *How to Be a Positive Leader* are distinctive. First, the book takes the perspective that small actions by leaders can and do have big impact. The authors identify small actions that make a big difference in the potential for enlarging capacities for positive impact. Second, the book uses a dual lens, focusing on what leaders can do to expand their *own* capacities for excellence while they seed directives for sustaining the capacities for excellence through more organizational-level actions. Third, the book is inspirational. It invites leaders to see the possibilities for expanded and improved human capacities enabled by small actions.

Who Is This Book For?

We do not assume that you or other leaders require formal power to be positive leaders. In fact, we believe that leaders, inside and outside of formal organizational roles, have the power to change trajectories of excellence in organizations. They can unlock resources, foster positive relationships, tap into the good, and engage generative change. This book is written for anyone with aspirations to become a more positive leader: anyone who seeks to increase capacities for excellence. It offers important lessons for senior leaders in a corporation, middle managers, directors of a nonprofit, entrepreneurs, or individual contributors. Many of these lessons apply not only to the world of work but also to family and social life, as well as to involvement in community, civic, and volunteer activities.

Why This Book Now?

This book could not come at a better time because leaders—and all people in organizations—are being asked to do more with less. It is also a time when too many employees and leaders are less than fully engaged and not fully developing their potential. Against the backdrop of the squeeze for greater performance and languishing work engagement, leaders need new visions and new actions for how to increase individual and organizational capacities for excellence. The purpose of this book is to ignite and to inspire new possibilities for action as a positive leader.

Who Is Offering Insights?

We have assembled some of the most respected thought leaders in the vibrant field of positive organizational scholarship (POS) to offer their best evidence-based recommendations. They discuss how to be a positive leader, that is, how to bring out the best in themselves as leaders as well as in organizations. POS is the intellectual discipline behind the research grounding these chapters. We invited each scholar to identify and make the case for positive leadership using a "seed idea," which is a core action-based idea that expands possibilities for excellence in individuals or organizations. We use the image of a seed to emphasize that leadership actions can start out small but expand and grow capacities inside people and organizations. Each author also offers strategies for germinating the seed idea in organizations, along with examples of positive leaders in action. Together, the chapters provide a compelling mandate and enriched portfolio for positive leaders who wish to have big impact.

Four clusters of positive leader strategies form the structure of the book. The first cluster covers positive relationships as the keystone for positive leadership. Jane E. Dutton describes the power and strategies for building high-quality connections, Adam M. Grant advocates outsourcing inspiration through connecting people to their impact on others, and Shirli Kopelman and Ramaswami Mahalingam illuminate how to negotiate mindfully.

The second cluster focuses on ways positive leaders can unlock resources from within people, within relationships, and within teams by activating and expanding key renewable resources such as energy, initiative, optimism, meaning, and creative thinking. Three chapters address this approach to positive leadership: Gretchen M. Spreitzer and Christine Porath detail how to enable thriving at work, Laura Morgan Roberts describes how to cultivate positive identities, and Amy Wrzesniewski illuminates the power and practices of job crafting.

The third cluster focuses on how to lead positively by tapping into the good in people and in collectives. These chapters examine how leaders can foster the best of the human condition for individuals and for organizations as a whole. Kim Cameron explains how to activate virtuousness, David M. Mayer describes how to lead an ethical organization, and Robert E. Quinn and Anjan V. Thakor articulate how to create organizations of higher purpose.

A final cluster envisions positive leaders as change makers and unpacks how to think and act in ways that generate resourceful change. Resourceful change implies that leaders build strength and capability while they foster change. Oana Branzei articulates how to cultivate hope, Karen Golden-Biddle describes how to create micro-moves that engage people in change, Scott Sonenshein makes the case for how to foster resourcefulness during change, and Lynn Perry Wooten and Erika Hayes James focus on how to learn from crises.

Each chapter explains why the specific leadership approach produces positive impact by drawing on the most compelling research evidence. The chapters describe what leaders can do to make their leadership approach a reality for themselves and how to put the approach into practice within a work organization. Each chapter concludes with an example that documents how a specific leader or organization deployed this positive leadership approach. These examples capture a range of leader types, such as founders, senior leaders, and middle managers, from a variety of industries, such as health care and retail, and market conditions ranging from fast growth to decline. This book ignites possibilities for bringing out the best in work organizations and broadens any positive leader's repertoire of actions to create enduring and beneficial impacts.

We invite you to share this journey on the road to becoming a positive leader. We hope the ideas and practices shared will be a kind of oxygen for action for you to see how small actions can have big impact for you and your organization.

I

FOSTER POSITIVE RELATIONSHIPS

Relationships are a source of strength and connection, as well as a means by which a leader's work gets done. In this section, our contributors invite you to attend to the quality of the relationships you form and the means by which you form them as important levers for increasing your own capability for excellence and the capabilities of others. This section opens up possibilities for uplifts in motivation, engagement, and meaning for you and for others by creating relationships between people and the beneficiaries of their work. Finally, this section zooms in on interrelating in negotiation and guides you in how to work mindfully and productively with your emotions to create win-win outcomes. This section reveals a rich array of means by which fostering positive relationships for you and for others can boost capacities for excellence.

1

Build High-Quality Connections

Jane E. Dutton

Think of the last time an interaction at work literally lit you up. Before the interaction, you may have felt depleted, tired, or simply neutral. After the interaction, even if it was brief, you had greater energy and capability for action. This sense of heightened energy is real, and it is an important indicator that you are engaged in a high-quality connection (HQC). Other signs include a sense of mutuality and positive regard. In HQCs, people feel attuned to one another and experience a sense of worth and value. HQCs are critical building blocks for bringing out the best in people and organizations. The seed for this chapter is that leaders can bring out the best in themselves and others by building more high-quality connections at work. They also can design and implement practices, structures, and cultures fostering high-quality connection building throughout the organization and beyond.

The Value of High-Quality Connections

High-quality connections contribute to individual flourishing and to team and organizational effectiveness. These forms of connecting call forth positive emotions that are literally life-giving. Barbara Fredrickson, who studies the power of positive emotions in connection, suggests these moments of connection start people on an upward spiral of growth and fulfillment.[1] For leaders, tapping into the power of high-quality connections means taking seriously the evidence that this form of person-to-person interrelating is at the root of critical individual and collective capabilities. The following are just some of the benefits of high-quality connections:

1. People who have HQCs are physically and psychologically healthier.[2]
2. Higher-quality connections enhance a person's physiological resources.[3]
3. People in higher-quality connections tend to have greater cognitive functioning.[4] High-quality connections also broaden people's capacities for thinking.[5]
4. People in higher-quality connections are better at knowing who to trust—and who not to trust.
5. When people are in HQCs at work, they tend to exhibit more learning behaviors.[6]
6. When people are in higher-quality connections at work and when top management teams have greater-quality connections between them, they tend to be more resilient (i.e., bouncing back from setbacks more effectively).[7]
7. When people are in HQCs at work, they tend to be more committed and more involved, and they display more organizational citizenship behaviors.[8]
8. When people are in higher-quality connections at work and teams have higher-quality connections, individuals and team members are more creative.[9]
9. At the organizational level, more HQCs enable greater overall employee commitment and engagement at work.[10]

10. At the organizational level, more higher-quality connections enable relational coordination, marked by shared knowledge, shared goals, and mutual respect, which is associated with greater organizational effectiveness in terms of greater efficiency and higher-quality performance.[11]

The beauty of high-quality connections is that they do not require significant time to build because they can be created in the moment. Meaningful investments of time and attention can further strengthen quality.

Strategies for Building High-Quality Connections

As a leader who wishes to ignite the best in yourself and in others, you have a range of potent options for building more HQCs with others and for designing organizations fostering this form of interconnecting.[12] We begin with your own interpersonal possibilities and invite you to consider four distinct pathways, or types of actions, to make workplace interactions more likely to yield high-quality connections.

Pathway 1: Respectfully Engage Others

Small acts matter in conferring worth to another person. Respect, or honoring another person's existence or value, is a state that is created in interaction with other people. Respect is not something we can grant ourselves; rather, it is a quality of experienced valuing from another person coming from subtle or direct messages of appreciation and worth. Respectfully engaging another person is accomplished through behaviors that signal that one person exists and is important in the eyes of another. There are at least three different moves that leaders can engage in to respectfully engage others and to foster the building of HQCs.

One of the most potent ways is through presence, or psychologically and/or physically being attentive to another person's existence. Conveying presence takes effort for leaders, as hectic schedules, technological demands, and physical demands are just some of the barriers to communicating to another person they possess significance and value. Conveying presence means showing up bodily for another person, whether in someone's physical or virtual presence. Our bodies provide rich and revealing displays, signaling whether we are present— or absent. We explicitly remind others with our displays to stay attuned to and to be with another person. For example, turning off one's phone or physically moving away from the computer can be potent signals that one is ready, present, and receptive to connection with another person.

Respectful engagement also happens through effective listening and communicating supportively. If leaders can engage these two critical aspects of respectful engagement, high-quality connections result. Effective listening requires both empathy and active engagement. Empathy implies being tuned into what another person is saying so that one can imagine what the other person is feeling and meaning. Being an active listener means being genuinely responsive to the person who is speaking through moves such as paraphrasing or summarizing what another person is saying, asking questions, or soliciting feedback.[13] Supportive communication is a quality of communication that involves attending both to what is said and to how it is said in ways that provide direct, descriptive, and actionable information that another person can hear and use.[14] Supportive communication involves making requests and not demands,[15] which invites a form of engagement that is voluntary and receptive, leading to a higher quality connection.

Pathway 2: Task-Enable Others

At the heart of task enabling is the core idea that higher-quality connections form if we facilitate another's success or performance on a task or a goal. When we task-enable others, they sense our interpersonal investment and desire to help, which opens them to an HQC. Of all the options for building high-quality connections, task enabling is often the method most explicitly recognized by work organizations. For example, when organizations assign mentors or coaches to facilitate another person's development, they are formalizing a task-enabling role. They are betting it will make a difference for a person's performance or growth. However, most task enabling happens informally, when one person reaches out to help another because they sense that they have something to offer and can make a difference. Critical and often-used enabling resources include emotional support, encouragement, recognition, guidance, task information, and flexibility. The most effective task enabling involves matching the resources provided to the task at hand and the specific style and needs of the person. Accordingly, task enabling often requires soliciting feedback about whether the help being provided meets the need. Sustained task enabling builds and supports HQCs, and works best when a continuous learning process is in place. Both people are soliciting and providing feedback that matches enabling resources with the particular needs of the person engaged in the task.

Pathway 3: Trust Others

Trusting another person is a pathway for building HQCs. Although a well-worn and frequent prescription, trusting others at work can sometimes be difficult. Trusting means being vulnerable and relying on another person to follow through on their commitments. Trusting involves paying attention both to what you say and what you do, as well as to what you do *not* say and do. For example, good trusting moves include sharing resources, granting access, delegating responsibility, being open, and seeking input. However, trusting to build HQCs also means *not* monitoring and controlling excessively, ignoring input, acting inconsistently, or accusing another of bad intentions. Trust is hard work, especially if one has grown up or worked in contexts where it is a rare or misused condition. In addition, if trust is broken, it can be difficult and time consuming to repair. Despite these challenges, trusting moves are potent contributors to high-quality connections that make interrelating smoother, more efficient, and more enjoyable.

Pathway 4: Play

All species play, and humans at work are no exception. What is sometimes overlooked is the importance of play in building connections. Moments of play are moments of exploration and interaction, often building new knowledge and broadening action possibilities. They frequently evoke positive emotions, which open people up to new and generative ways of interacting. Play at work is often associated with innovation and creativity because it fosters new knowledge and develops cognitive skills.[16] However, the role of play in building connections—especially ones where people are energized and sense mutual regard—is often missed or underestimated. Play at work takes numerous forms. Some units or organizations institutionalize play through team-building activities, volunteer opportunities, or simply by having play supplies, such as ping-pong tables or basketball courts, readily available. Leaders and employees can enact numerous moves to engage play, either in formal forums such as meetings or at informal gatherings such as celebrations. What is most important to remember about this pathway is that it exists as a powerful and low-investment option for building HQCs.

Designing Organizations That Foster Building and Maintaining High-Quality Connections

Leaders have multiple means for creating a work context that encourages both the creation and the sustenance of high-quality connections.[17] Leading for sustainable excellence in an organization means taking actions to create and to institutionalize a context where HQCs are the norm and the expected form of human-to-human interrelating for employees, customers, suppliers, and all relevant organizational stakeholders. Leaders have at least three design choices that are likely to cultivate and support high-quality connections.

Reward High-Quality Connection Building and Relational Skills

Leaders have several options for formally and informally rewarding effective connection building. Some leaders create team-based awards where a portion of an employee's incentives are tied to collective as well as individual performance. The use of team or group incentives focuses attention and motivation around collaboration, which fosters the building of high-quality connections.[18] Some leaders also encourage HQCs through the creation of spot awards or peer-controlled rewards, which allow for the recognition of excellence based on a peer's contribution to collective performance. Southwest Airlines is one organization that deploys these types of incentives, and their use is one of the reasons analysts see them as highly effective in relational coordination.[19] Finally, leaders can encourage the building of relational skills (e.g., social intelligence or effective helping) as part of talent development, providing further incentives for creating and building a workforce that is sensitive to and invested in bettering their capacity to build and to sustain HQCs.

Build High-Quality Connection Routines and Practices

Routines and practices are repeated activities and ways of doing things that become typical and normative in any organization. Often taken for granted, these ways of acting may come to typify an organization, but they can be potent contributors to high-quality connection building. Multiple routines and practices foster HQC building. For example, some organizations explicitly select employees who have relationship-building attitudes and competencies. Others routinize significant peer involvement in employee selection as another means for building HQCs when a person begins their organizational membership. Still others utilize onboarding practices that are explicitly designed to foster rapid and significant quality connecting for newcomers.[20] Use of relational onboarding practice means giving priority to opportunities that enable newcomers to connect with the appropriate people, instead of overwhelming them with information. Finally, practices used during routine meetings can be potent means for fostering connections. For example, making sure people are introduced in ways that equip others to engage and to trust them, and facilitating people to be well prepared for meetings, are simple but potent practices to bring about high-quality connection building.

Model and Value High-Quality Connection Building

It is well known that leaders' behaviors model and influence what is appropriate conduct for organizational members and thus are critical shapers of an organization's culture. Consequently, if leaders wish to foster HQC building, they need to conduct themselves with this mindset and behavioral repertoire in much of what they do. Leaders can convey values and priorities that elevate the importance of connection building, setting the tone for others to see these behaviors as important and valued activities. Researchers writing about the impact of leadership on interpersonal caring and on the creation of caring cultures in organizations identify various leadership behaviors that can shape organizational-level caring (and provide support for the building of HQCs).[21] As an everyday example, leaders can act to be present, use face-to-face contact, and engage in active listening, demonstrating knowledge, understanding, and caring for the needs of various organizational constituencies. But leaders can also model values and behaviors in crisis, affecting members' motivation to connect in high-quality ways with others. Leaders' actions in the wake of the September 11, 2001, attacks on the United States were important shapers of members' connection-building activities.[22] As an example of crisis leadership, Phil Lynch, president of Reuters America, headquartered in New York City, took immediate actions to continuously and personally communicate and to be present with all his employees as they wrestled with both human losses and technical challenges associated with that day's horrific events. Leaders' actions toward others during times of duress and challenge leave an indelible impression of appropriate and desired ways of interrelating that last far beyond the immediate circumstances.

Putting It All Together

Bringing out the best in oneself, and in others, means paying attention to and investing in the quality of the social fabric where we are growing and performing. The quality of the social fabric is built one interaction at a time. When we make these interactions high quality, we build personal strength, and we also strengthen and enrich the fabric that sustains, grows, and facilitates others.

BUILDING HIGH-QUALITY CONNECTIONS WITH CLIENTS: THE CASE OF WESTON SOLUTIONS

Weston Solutions (hereafter Weston) is a global employee-owned firm delivering "integrated environmental, sustainability, property redevelopment, energy, and construction solutions for clients" (http://www.we stonsolutions.com/about/index.htm). High-quality connections with clients are critical for Weston's strategic success because of the large financial stakes involved with each client engagement and the importance of client engagements for the company's reputation.

Weston's management intentionally cultivates awareness and commitment to the importance of building and helping others build HQCs with clients. The company provides training on HQC building for all project managers (PMs). An interview study with the PMs revealed three benefits of HQCs with clients. At the firm level, HQCs with clients yield financial benefits by reducing the need for price renegotiations during contract renewals, increasing contract renewal rates, and maintaining sole source supplier status. A PM explained that with HQCs, "we get challenging projects which are more profitable." At the project level, HQCs with clients keep engagements flexible and bring in more diverse work, while making client work more enjoyable. In addition, project managers report extensive personal and professional learning when client connections are high quality.

As leaders, PMs foster HQCs with clients using five strategies: (1) having frequent, open communication with clients with some regular face-to-face contact; (2) personalizing the client relationship by connecting outside of work; (3) committing to always exceeding client expectations; (4) making early admission of mistakes or missed deadlines; and (5) being open, honest, dependable, transparent, and acting with integrity. Project managers looked for what would be home runs for clients and then tried to hit the ball "out of the park" to achieve quality. As one PM said, "You ask the client, 'Okay, for this particular assignment, what would a home run be for you?'" Another PM reflected the same core belief about hitting home runs: "It demonstrates to our customers and our clients that we're willing to do whatever it takes to make them successful. And at the end of the day, we're going to give them more than they paid for."

TWEETS

Did you know that short, momentary interactions with people at work are like vitamins that strengthen and fortify you throughout your day?

Expand your repertoires of ways to build high-quality connections by doing more task enabling, respectfully engaging, trusting, and playing more with others.

Have you considered how to design your team, unit, or organization to foster quality connections? Your life and performance depend upon it.

2

Outsource Inspiration

Adam M. Grant

When employee motivation is lacking, many leaders grab the loudspeaker. They stand up, deliver an inspiring speech, and hope for the best. There is reason to believe, though, that it is often more effective for leaders to take a backseat. Leaders can accomplish more by outsourcing inspiration to end users—the people who benefit from the organization's products and services. It is a different way of motivating and engaging employees, one that recognizes the power of leaders' actions to speak louder than their words. By making connections to end users, leaders can enable employees to identify their past and potential contributions, injecting greater meaning into work.

Why Outsourcing Inspiration Matters

Meaningful work is a cornerstone of motivation.[1] For many years, researchers have recognized the motivating potential of task significance—doing work that affects the well-being of others.[2] But all too often, employees do work that makes a difference but never have the chance to see or to meet the people affected by their work.

Ten years ago, I found this sign in a call center at the University of Michigan: "Doing a good job here is like wetting your pants in a dark suit. You get a warm feeling, but no one else notices." A natural solution was to help the callers see how the money they raised was making a difference. At the beginning of a calling shift, a leader described how the funds contributed to new buildings, faculty and staff salaries, and—perhaps most importantly—the Michigan football and basketball teams.

My team's role was to track the effects, and there were none. The callers did not work any harder or more productively. We realized that it might be the right message, but it was coming from the wrong source. When a leader articulated the importance of the work, the callers were suspicious. After all, the leader had an ulterior motive of convincing them to work harder.

To overcome this problem, we randomly divided the callers among three groups. For the face-to-face contact group, we invited a scholarship student, Will, to talk firsthand about the importance of the work. He spent five minutes with the callers, explaining that their work had helped to fund his scholarship, that it had changed his life, and that he wanted to thank them for their efforts. Other callers read a letter from him without any direct contact, and the remaining callers were in a control group with no exposure to Will.

Over the next month, on average, the callers who met Will spiked 142 percent in weekly minutes on the phone and 171 percent in weekly revenue. The callers who merely read the letter or had no contact with him showed no changes in effort or productivity. A five-minute interaction with a single scholarship recipient was enough to dramatically increase motivation and effectiveness.[3] Those callers who met Will developed a stronger sense that their work made a difference, felt more valued and appreciated—instead of rejected and disrespected by alumni—and recognized that other scholarship students were depending on them. Once they realized that their work could be so valuable to others, they became motivated to work harder. They also gained new information that enabled them to work smarter, sharing scholarship stories on the phone with alumni.

In total, we replicated the effect five times with different callers and scholarship students. In one case, a short interaction with a scholarship recipient boosted individual callers' weekly revenue by more than 400 percent, from weekly averages of under $412 to over $2,083.[4] In contrast, there were no significant changes in callers' behavior or performance when leaders and managers delivered the same information[5] or when we invited a former caller to address the personal benefits of the job for learning and career advancement.[6] The boost in motivation appears to be unique to seeing firsthand how one's work is beneficial to other people.

This effect holds true in a wide range of health and safety jobs. Consider the following evidence:

- **Nurses.** When assembling surgical kits, nurses who met the health-care practitioners who would use the kits worked 64 percent more minutes, completed more than twice as many pieces, and made 15 percent fewer errors than nurses in a control group who had no beneficiary contact.[7]
- **Radiologists.** When the patient's photo was included in their file, radiologists wrote 29 percent longer reports and achieved 46 percent greater diagnostic accuracy in scanning exams.[8]
- **Lifeguards.** After reading stories about other lifeguards performing rescues, lifeguards increased their average

monthly hours worked by 43 percent, and supervisors rated them as 21 percent more helpful. These effects were driven by perceiving the job as having a greater impact on swimmers and feeling more valued by swimmers.[9]

- **Physicians and nurses.** Merely mentioning that hand hygiene protects patients against diseases increased soap and gel usage by more than 45 percent and hand washing by more than 10 percent.[10]
- **Pharmaceutical employees.** Hearing a patient talk for an hour about experiences with treating a disease significantly increased engagement scores on a survey two months later. Employees reported greater pride in the organization, a stronger sense of commitment and willingness to go beyond the requirements of the job, and a heightened belief in the meaningfulness of the organization's vision in their daily jobs.[11]

Research also shows that exposure to the impact of one's work can motivate greater effort and performance in more mundane tasks:[12]

- **Giving feedback.** When making suggestions to improve job application cover letters for a student who needed a job, people who briefly saw the student worked 18 percent longer than those who did not see the student.
- **Editing.** When correcting grammar in an international student's research paper, people who saw a video of a student who benefited from this type of feedback in the past caught 34 percent more errors than those who saw a video of the leader describe the same information, and 37 percent more errors than a control group who saw no video.

- **Generating a marketing campaign.** When creating a pitch for a new service, people who read a letter from a customer who benefited from the service developed ideas that were rated by experts as 11 percent higher in quality than ideas from people who read an identical letter from a leader describing the customer's experience.

Strategies for Connecting to Your Own Impact

In light of these motivational benefits, what can you do to increase your own awareness of your impact? Over the past decade, I've encountered four different ways that leaders can connect the dots between what they do on the job and its consequences for others.

1. **Pay periodic visits to end users.** In many organizations, leaders have little contact with the end users who benefit from their work. Busy schedules make it difficult to rank trips to see clients and customers as a priority, and this often means an impoverished understanding of the impact of your work. By making it a priority to spend time with end users, you can gather information about their needs and your contributions. At IBM, for example, Lou Gerstner required his top fifty senior executives to visit at least five of IBM's largest customers in a three-month period.[13] As one observer explains, "That empathic connection to real-world customers helped managers to see whether a particular decision added value for customers or destroyed it."[14]

2. **Seek internal feedback.** As a leader, much of your impact is on people inside the organization. It is surprisingly common, though, for leaders to lack awareness of how their work makes a difference in the lives of employees. Evidence suggests that

one of the most reliable steps for solving this problem is to meet twice per month with each of your employees.[15] Regular meetings serve to increase trust and communication quality, enabling employees to more clearly articulate the impact of your relationship. (Interestingly, whereas many leaders view such meetings as time-sapping distractions, research suggests that they actually save time, in part by reducing interruptions by up to 80 percent—employees save their requests until meetings.)[16] At each meeting, it is worth asking what you have done that has been the most and the least helpful—and how employees and mentees have implemented the advice and suggestions that you gave in the previous meeting.

3. **Keep a journal about your contributions.** It is easy to lose sight of how your actions make a difference. In high-pressure jobs, with many strategic priorities and interactions, many leaders are too busy doing work to reflect on its significance. One small step for combating this challenge is to keep a journal about how you have made a difference. In an experiment with fund-raising callers, Jane Dutton and I found that writing about contributions for less than an hour per week was enough to boost hourly calls by more than 29 percent.[17] The journaling process appeared to reinforce their sense that their jobs mattered and to strengthen their identities as helpful, giving individuals, energizing them to contribute more. But timing matters in two ways. First, the boost does not always occur right away: evidence from firefighters and rescue workers suggests that on days where they have made a big difference, they experience gains in energy only after they have had time to reflect.[18] Second, research indicates that journaling about positive experiences is more beneficial once a week rather than once a day, likely because writing weekly feels more novel and allows time for a few meaningful contributions to add up.[19]

4. **Become an end user.** One of the easiest ways to understand how your work makes a difference for clients or customers is to become a client or customer. Using your organization's products or services can shed new light on the consequences of your job. For example, at Patagonia, founder Yvon Chouinard encourages leaders and employees to field-test outdoor sports products, and at Four Seasons Hotels, new employees are invited to do a "familiarization stay" overnight in their own hotels.[20] The more experience you gain with your organization's offerings, the more you can internalize the end user's perspective and understand the past and future impact of your work.

Connecting Employees to Their Impact

Beyond seeing your own impact more clearly, you can take the initiative to help employees across the organization see how their efforts make a difference. Leaders at several innovative organizations have introduced three kinds of strategies that serve this purpose.

1. **Make the face-to-face connection.** The most direct way of connecting employees to their impact is to invite end users to visit the organization.[21] At John Deere, many employees who built tractors had no interaction with the customers who would one day drive the tractors. Leaders decided to invite farmers who bought their first tractors to bring their families to the factory. Employees who worked on those tractors come to congratulate the farmers, give them a gold key, and see the joy on their faces as they turn the key to start the ignition. At Medtronic, engineers who design medical devices and salespeople who sell them to hospitals are able to see their impact at the company's annual holiday party. Six patients share their

stories about how the company's products have transformed their lives. Many employees break down into tears and walk away with an enriched understanding of the purpose behind their jobs.

2. **Encourage employees to swap stories.** In situations where it is not easy to facilitate face-to-face interactions, an alternative is to invite employees to share their own stories of making a difference. For example, at Merrill Lynch teams start weekly meetings by opening the floor for employees to relay experiences about helping clients, and at Ritz-Carlton hotels, employees have daily fifteen-minute meetings to exchange "wow" stories about how they have gone above and beyond the call of duty to benefit customers. When employees hear stories about impact from their colleagues, they can become more aware of the significance of their past contributions and recognize greater potential to make future contributions.

3. **Become a linking pin.** Giving end users the microphone does not mean watching the game from the sidelines. As a leader, you serve as a linking pin[22] to fill the gap between employees and end users. By leveraging your network, you can often find clients, customers, patients, and other beneficiaries of your organization's products and services who have novel stories to share. Further, recent studies show that among nurses[23] and fund-raising callers,[24] meeting end users is even more powerful when it happens in tandem with an inspiring speech from leaders. When you articulate your vision, you can invite end users to help bring the vision to life. At Medtronic's annual party, for example, senior leaders describe Medtronic's mission in conjunction with testimonials from patients. Along with connecting employees to end users, you can build a bridge between end users' specific stories and the organization's broader vision.

Putting It All Together

Outsourcing inspiration may sound like common sense, but it is not common practice. Surprisingly few leaders take the initiative to show how the organization's day-to-day work has meaningful, lasting benefits to other people. By forging these connections, it is possible to create work environments that are infused with richer meaning, deeper relationships, and greater productivity.

OUTSOURCING INSPIRATION AT WELLS FARGO

At Wells Fargo, manager Ben Soccorsy took over a low-interest personal loan product. For five years, the product group was languishing, having failed to grow the business. Soccorsy knew the loan had rescued some customers from severe debt; in one case, a customer facing eighteen years of debt was able to become debt-free in a third of the time. Nevertheless, bankers were detached from this impact on customers. "You have 70 million customers and 200 loan products, and you're busy in meetings and pulling information in Excel. It's really hard to create that connectivity: How does that end up helping people?"

Soccorsy decided to reposition the loan as a pathway to getting out of debt. His aim was to connect the product to everyday customer needs. He wanted to communicate the message to a wide range of bankers efficiently, but also powerfully. Knowing that videos were an important part of banker training, he proposed to create videos that conveyed how the low-interest loans had saved customers from debt.

Initially, some insiders were skeptical. "They didn't understand why we would take my precious time and other people's precious time to do storytelling or make a video. Didn't I have a business to run?" To overcome resistance, Soccorsy highlighted how the initiative was intertwined with the vision of the company, which focused on helping customers succeed financially. After gaining internal support, he created a proposal and a budget. Then his team began reaching out to bankers and customers to identify powerful stories from around the United States and filmed five videos. A typical video started with a customer problem, profiled the banker-customer interaction, and showed the consequences for the customer. "Customers felt like they had a massive weight lifted off their shoulders," Soccorsy says, and the videos displayed "the raw emotion with customers when bankers helped them find some light at the end of the tunnel."

When bankers watched the videos, "it was like a light switch turned on," Soccorsy says. "They really were connecting the impact on the customer to their day-to-day work. Bankers realized the impact their work could have—that this loan can really make a difference in customers' lives. It was a really compelling motivator. They gave the whole effort another look. It humanized our work and how important it is to customers. It's a way to connect the dots—a secret weapon that we don't use enough."[25] The product became a major source of growth for the company, and doubled in size in the span of just a few years.

TWEETS

Outsource inspiration: instead of motivating employees with your words, give the microphone to customers.

Leaders are linking pins: they connect employees to the people who find their work meaningful.

Meeting one person who benefits from your work can boost your productivity by more than 400 percent.

3

Negotiate Mindfully

*Shirli Kopelman and
Ramaswami Mahalingam*

When you negotiate with people inside or outside your organization, are you able to align your emotions with your strategy? Are you able to engage in productive conversations, leading you and others toward desired positive outcomes? Many conversations you lead at work constitute a negotiation over resources. Sometimes the resource is money, but more frequently, leaders negotiate timelines, roles, responsibilities, or ideas on how to move forward. Because negotiations inherently involve both a common goal, such as joint value creation, as well as personal agendas, such as individual value claiming, they can be emotionally challenging. How do you manage the emotions that surface in such conversations? In this chapter, we offer strategies for mindful emotion management and explore relationship capacities enabling leaders to negotiate mindfully[1] and cocreate extraordinary value for all.

The Value of Negotiating Mindfully

Research suggests that emotions can challenge or facilitate negotiation processes and outcomes.[2] Positive emotions, such as happiness, or negative ones, such as anger, can be helpful in a negotiation, but can also be counterproductive. The key is to align emotions with strategic goals, which requires displaying your emotions strategically and responding strategically to the emotions displayed by others. Such emotion management is especially challenging in complex, mixed-motive tasks such as negotiations. Although many wrongly assume negotiation contexts are purely competitive,[3] negotiations are both a cooperative and competitive social interaction.[4] Negotiations provide opportunities for synergistic value to be created, but this value is distributed between negotiators. Functioning within this tension of simultaneously being motivated to create and to claim value necessitates sophisticated cooperative and competitive strategies that are well established in negotiation literature.[5] But less frequently examined are the emotional dynamics resulting from engaging in both cooperation *and* competition. When you negotiate, you might feel happy about cooperating to explore synergies and at the same time feel anxious about how much of this value you will be able to secure for your team.[6]

A mindful approach enables emotion management in negotiations. Mindfulness is a practice that positive leaders can adopt, as well as foster in their organizations, to excel in negotiations. In everyday parlance, it refers to being reflective, deliberate, and wise. It is considered a process of self-reflection, enabling attention and learning. Research on mindful attention and reflection has provided valuable insights and made significant contributions to a growing body of psychology and organizational behavior research.[7] Our definition of mindfulness is broader. Leaders need not only to practice self-reflection but to cultivate an awareness of openness and presence in the context of interpersonal, or relational, dynamics. Therefore, to negotiate mindfully goes beyond a cognitive capacity to be in the present moment, to the development of a positive relational presence.

The relational capacities of mindfulness enable emotion management and fuel a positive approach to negotiations, defined by Kopelman as maximizing sustainable individual and joint economic outcomes as well as promoting individual and organizational well-being.[8]

Relational Mindfulness

As a leader who would like to productively manage emotions in the context of negotiations, you need to cultivate relational mindfulness by being (1) balanced, (2) joyful and kind, and (3) compassionate.

Enabler 1: Be Balanced

Balance, or equanimity, is a critical relational capacity. A balanced approach, not only with one's own emotions, but also with the emotional dynamics experienced in the context of relationships, is essential for successful negotiation. It requires being nonjudgmental and nonreactive to your own emotions and to those displayed by others. To be nonjudgmental suggests accepting the present emotions as your current reality, a reality that can be changed, and yet currently "is." For example, you may feel extremely anxious anticipating a complex negotiation. Even if you wish you had not gotten anxious, you are experiencing anxiety. To be nonreactive suggests not internally responding to this feeling of anxiety, whether by judging yourself for experiencing the emotion or by acting on the emotion. Balance requires metaphorically viewing emotions simply as they are: emotions. You cultivate an awareness of emotions while you experience them and notice the constant changes in how you experience your emotions.

Balance enables you as a leader to observe and be "with your emotions," not "in your emotions."[9]

Enabler 2: Be Joyful and Kind

Relational mindfulness goes beyond being cooperative. It includes a capacity to celebrate when others do well. Often, people feel jealous when they compare themselves to others, and such negative social comparisons lead to resentment toward others' happiness. To rejoice with the happiness of others strengthens your social ties in any negotiation. Beyond being able to experience sympathetic joy in the positive outcomes of others, relational mindfulness includes being friendly and kind to others.[10] Kindness is not a passive state, but an active practice. Cultivating kindness toward others encompasses intentional thoughts, feelings, and behavior. An example is the loving-kindness foundational meditation, which includes consciously sending *metta* (a Pali word for loving-kindness) to cultivate kindness toward others. Research shows that loving-kindness meditation fosters positive emotions toward oneself and others and promotes physical and psychological well-being.[11]

Enabler 3: Be Compassionate

Compassion refers to your capacity to empathize with the pain of others. Empathy and perspective taking are critical to cultivate compassion. But compassion goes beyond these thoughts and feelings. Compassion refers not only to your capacity to feel others' suffering or pain but also to your capacity to take some action to alleviate others' pain. Compassion helps you cultivate patience to regulate emotions toward those who are suffering and also toward those who might be hurting you. It is critical in organizational contexts.[12] Compassion, when directed toward yourself, also helps you to accept your own shortcomings and manage associated emotions.

Overall, a mindful relational presence suggests a deep positive connection with yourself *and* with your negotiation partners. In the context of negotiations, relational mindfulness enables consideration and alignment of the emotional dynamics you *and* others experience as you explore opportunities to cocreate value. It is not an outcome but a process through which negotiators story their relationship. Leaders who mindfully narrate, rather than be narrated by the emotions that surface in negotiations, create more possibilities to unlock resources that cocreate and maximize value.

Strategies for Managing Emotions

Self-narration is a process that enables you to mindfully and strategically manage emotions during a negotiation.[13] Mindfulness enables nonjudgmental and nonreactive observing and accepting your emotions with positive relational presence. Strategically refers to aligning emotions with cooperative and competitive actions that help you generatively cocreate and appropriately allocate negotiated resources, while also building positive business relationships.

The self-narration process includes three strategies to manage emotions in real time during a negotiation. A scientific understanding of emotions may be helpful to see why. In general, there are three critical phases in moving from noticing social triggers to experiencing a full emotional response:[14] (1) basic perception of stimuli triggering the emotion, such as seeing your teams' reports; (2) cognitive appraisal or interpretation of this data, such as interpreting these as extraordinary performance; and (3) an onset of physiological experiences, such as feeling an increased heart rate and excitement. It is possible to intervene at each or any of these phases by managing the emotions as you experience them. By mindfully and strategically redirecting your attention, reinterpreting information, and/ or reconfiguring how your body responds, self-narration enables you to leverage both positive and negative emotions. For example, perhaps you were only mildly happy at first and wished you were more excited about your team's extraordinary performance. Appropriately increasing or decreasing the intensity of your emotions can help you achieve your negotiation goals.

Three strategies will help you to suppress or to intensify an emotion you wish to experience differently. Imagine you feel intensely angry during a meeting when a project manager (PM) in your leadership team lays out a plan you think is completely unreasonable. You wish you did not feel so angry. It would help you negotiate a more appropriate timeline. What could you do? The following are examples of the three strategies for emotion management in this situation.

Strategy 1: Mindfully Notice Emotionally Incongruent Triggers in the Environment

While listening to the PM utter the words "three months," you also notice she directs her gaze toward someone seated at the other end of the conference table. As your gaze moves across the room, you also notice the excitement of her team, aligning together to meet an important organizational project. You remember she had successfully completed past projects in what you considered warp speed.

Strategy 2: Mindfully Reinterpret Emotional Triggers

You reinterpret the event, realizing the PM's goal was to impress someone on the other side of the table. You consider whether three months represents an ambitious anchor rather than an overly aggressive delivery date, and therefore is a solid negotiation strategy.

Strategy 3: Mindfully Modify Physiological Reaction to Emotional Triggers

As you continue to listen to the PM's pitch, you intentionally—and inconspicuously—change the grasp on your pencil from a grip to gently holding it like a violin bow. At the same time that you consider interpreting the goal to be "ambitious" rather than "aggressive," you feel a sigh of relief. At the end of that sigh, you slowly inhale as much oxygen as possible into your abdomen to boost the effect. You make sure nobody notices, as it could be misinterpreted or trigger an emotional reaction in others.

The order of the interventions is fluid and not necessarily linear. You can iteratively intervene, beginning with any of the strategies. You can generate a cycle of interventions, enabling you to suppress or to intensify an emotion. The interventions are productive, aligned with your negotiation goals, and therefore your emotions are now both mindfully and strategically displayed.[15]

You may find yourself automatically self-evaluating when you experience strong emotions that you believe are inappropriate or counterproductive. These thoughts can make things worse because they lead you to self-ruminate and repeatedly experience the emotion you wish you did not feel. You intensify, rather than diminish, the emotions. Ironically, you may then criticize yourself for self-evaluating and experience even stronger negative emotions. Letting go is very difficult. But accepting your emotions, such as your anger, is even more difficult. To negotiate mindfully requires exactly that: nonjudgmental acceptance and compassion toward yourself. You may not be proud of what you feel or comfortable with emotions others express. However, these emotions may be a reality that paradoxically needs to be accepted as is, in order to change it. Mindfulness enables being nonjudgmental and nonreactive, therefore accepting the reality of the present. The relational capacities of mindfulness go beyond mere acceptance by helping you to direct and to manage emotions in a positive and productive way. Mindfulness thus enables the three strategies for emotion management.

Putting It All Together

To negotiate mindfully, leaders need to narrate the emotional landscape of cooperative and competitive negotiations by cultivating equanimity, joyful kindness, and compassion. These relational capacities enable mindful and strategic emotion management, leading to successful negotiation outcomes. Adopting a positive approach to negotiations,[16] leaders bring out the best in themselves and others by cultivating relational mindfulness and narrating emotions to cocreate extraordinary economic outcomes and individual and organizational well-being.

CULTIVATING RELATIONAL MINDFULNESS AT REVIVA AND CELIA

Amos is a co-owner of Reviva and Celia, a famous restaurant located in the residential Israeli neighborhood of Ramat Hasharon. The place is known for its fabulous pastries, food, and service. For many years, it has been one of the country's most successful restaurants. Amos leads the restaurant's strategy, staff, and customer relations. He negotiates in all of these roles, mindfully cocreating value while keeping an eye on the profitability of the business. Amos negotiates every detail of running his business to perfection. Yet the success of the restaurant is equally attributable to the quality of the food, led by co-owner Reviva, as it is to Amos's relationally mindful negotiation skills.

"Always crowded, yet feels intimate," is a common theme echoed in reviews of the business. The restaurant is known as a place for celebrity sightings and the "who's who" of Israel's business, political, and entertainment world. Although it operates in a very direct and frequently confrontational Israeli culture, Amos mindfully negotiates and manages his emotions to cocreate value and generate a genuine experience that is difficult to replicate. If you are familiar with the restaurant industry, you know that customers and proprietors can experience strong emotions that may or may not be aligned with positive business outcomes. Amos skillfully narrates his own emotions and strategically responds to emotions displayed by his customers.

Amos is balanced and kind. He rejoices when others are pleased and is compassionate. He teaches his staff to do the same. "We didn't invent anything new," Amos says.[17] "Many neighborhood cafes have regular customers, but we took it to perfection because we are deliberate, genuine, and consistent." For example, every new waiter learns the name of the businessman who always sits at the corner table, who is sitting next to them on a particular day, and what they are celebrating. The staff knows the name of the businesswoman sitting at the far-away table and whether she had a good day on the stock market. It's strategy, but it's based on his personality and philosophy of life.

In Asian culture, a beautiful metaphor represents his mindful and deliberate presence: "like a water droplet on a lotus leaf." The water droplet on the lotus leaf stays, maintaining its shape. It never sticks to the surface, yet it is on the leaf. Amos is there, and together with his staff, provides the perfect leaf. As a customer, you feel like you are the *only* water droplet on the leaf. Your needs are maintained, respected, and fostered. His emotions are aligned with a mindful inter-being that deliberately maintains your privacy, yet provides a sense of intimacy and familiarity that makes everyone (staff, suppliers, and customers) belong and feel at home. And everyone always feels like they *got a great deal*. Some of his customers have been coming for twenty years, and their children and grandchildren also are now customers. In an industry with extremely high turnover, his staff is committed. Amos explains, "Something in the energy of how we interact as co-owners and as staff; it touches customers, and it's a fact, it works." Amos masterfully builds and fosters mindful and strategic business relationships and cocreates extraordinary negotiation outcomes.

TWEETS

Leaders can appropriately increase or decrease the intensity of emotions to cocreate positive relationships and maximize profits.

A positive approach to negotiations leverages mindful alignment of emotions through three iterative strategies.

To constructively manage emotions, leaders need to cultivate relational mindfulness.

II

UNLOCK RESOURCES
FROM WITHIN

As a leader you are often required to do more with less or to do better with no additional inputs. So the challenge becomes, how do you unlock valuable resources that already exist in yourself and in your organization to meet these new demands? This section's contributors offer three unique perspectives on how you can unlock valuable resources—resources that are often invisible and not yet accessed. One approach focuses on cultivating a state of thriving at work as a critical means for fostering energy, commitment, satisfaction, innovation, and health. A second perspective encourages leaders to construct positive identities as a means for generating vital resources such as more confidence, persistence, and creativity. The third approach encourages you to use the discretion that you (and others) have within a job to craft it to fit your strengths, passions, and values as a means for unleashing motivation and engagement. Being a positive leader implies being able to imagine and to act on the possibilities that there are always resources to be tapped—it just requires seeing and knowing how to unlock them.

4

Enable Thriving at Work

*Gretchen M. Spreitzer and
Christine Porath*

Reflect on a time when you felt most alive at work. What were you doing? Why does the experience stand out? More than likely, it was an experience marked not only by vitality but also by learning and growth—what we term "thriving at work." People experience growth and momentum marked by a sense of vitality while thriving at work; it is literally a feeling of energy, passion, and excitement—a spark.[1] In this chapter, we draw on the growing body of evidence to demonstrate why individuals and organizations should care about thriving. We also highlight strategies for individuals and leaders to enable more thriving at work.

Why Care? The Value of Thriving at Work

Organizations seek thriving employees. They report less burnout,[2] because the way in which they work generates, rather than depletes, resources.[3] In a thriving state, people exhibit better health, including fewer days of missed work and fewer visits to the doctor.[4] When people are thriving at work, they report more job satisfaction and organizational commitment.[5] Thriving individuals are apt to have a learning orientation—

experimenting with new ideas to propel their own learning. Thriving employees take initiative in developing their careers. Their supervisors rate them as high performers. And thriving employees exhibit more innovative work behavior, generating creative ideas, championing new ideas, and seeking out new ways of working.

Why do thriving employees achieve such positive outcomes? The vitality and learning dimensions suggest several mechanisms. First, the strong sense of feeling energized helps employees have the capacity to initiate proactive behaviors and persist amid daily challenges without burning out.[6] Second, the learning dimension helps individuals see that they are making progress and on a positive trajectory. They feel more confident that they will achieve positive outcomes. Third, the original thriving framework suggests these individuals do not view their work environment to be determined by external forces. Instead, they believe in cocreating their work environment to nurture more thriving. Through the process of cocreation, thriving employees create resources, including meaning, positive affect, high-quality connections, and knowledge, to enable continued thriving over time.[7] Together, these mechanisms provide the ingredients for sustained performance.

What Can I Do to Enhance My Own Thriving?

We offer four individual strategies to enable thriving at work. They are behavioral strategies anyone can engage in to kickstart their own thriving. Each of these strategies develops one of the previously mentioned key resources that are cocreated by thriving employees. Although the four strategies can be practiced in a piecemeal fashion, they are more potent if undertaken together.

Strategy 1: Craft Your Work to Be More Meaningful

Research suggests meaning is a key renewable resource to fuel thriving.[8] Having meaning energizes by creating purpose in one's work life, and with meaning, people care about their work.[9] A study of social service employees found those who reported more meaning in their work experienced more thriving.[10] Meaning boosts thriving by increasing focus, such as in getting work done, and in exploration behaviors, such as trying new things. In a study of high-tech workers, those who created more meaning in their work through reflection on how they make a difference experienced more vitality—one of the two dimensions of thriving at work.[11] Job crafting, a work redesign that individuals engage in to make work more fulfilling, may be a tool to generate more meaning at work (see Wrzesniewski, "Engage in Job Crafting," this volume).

Strategy 2: Look for Opportunities to Innovate

Knowledge is a second resource that fuels thriving. It builds feelings of competence, enabling vitality and learning. In that same study of high-tech workers, those who created opportunities for gaining new knowledge in their work, through setting goals or seeking feedback, possessed more vitality. The power of this strategy is further supported by self-determination theory, which articulates how feelings of competence enable vitality and growth at work.[12] "Mindful engagement" theory adds insight into how experimentation with new behaviors paired with periods of reflection ensures learning from those experiences.[13]

Strategy 3: Invest in Relationships That Energize

Relationships are a third resource that fuel thriving. Positive connections at work aid motivation, engagement, and well-being.

Social networks also enable learning, as they are the conduits for harnessing information and knowledge, resulting in thriving and performance. High-quality relationships are energizing (see Dutton, "Build High-Quality Connections," this volume). High-tech workers who invested in their relationships by making a colleague happy or showing gratitude experienced greater vitality. De-energizing relationships, on the other hand, take a tremendous toll on people. They have four times the negative effect as energizing relationships.[14] To increase thriving, be mindful of building high-quality relationships with energizers, and rejuvenating or disconnecting from de-energizing relationships.

Strategy 4: Take Care of Your Health through Energy Management

Positive affect is a fourth resource which can be increased through energy management.[15] These strategies draw on robust research that demonstrates how exercise and movement (cardiovascular and strength training), nutrition (balanced combinations of carbohydrates, proteins, and fat), and sleep (seven to eight hours per night) enhance positive moods during the workday. Our research also demonstrates the importance of these strategies for individuals who are seeking recovery when fatigued. The energy audit is one tool individuals can use to take a pulse on their energy and develop strategies for sustaining energy.[16]

What Practices Can My Organization Introduce to Enable Employees to Thrive?

In the previous section, we identified individual strategies for enhancing your own performance. In this section, we speak to the organizational practices that enable a more thriving workforce. Having a thriving workforce is proven to bring many benefits to an organization and its employees. But how does an organization integrate practices that enable its workforce to thrive more? Although potentially more complex to implement because they involve systems, these practices have incredible potential to transform your organization into a thriving enterprise. We are also happy to report that, for the most part, they have little financial cost to implement. However, they require discipline and are most potent when implemented in tandem to reinforce each other.

Practice 1: Sharing Information

People have more capacity to thrive when they understand how their work fits with the organization's mission and strategy. This practice builds feelings of competence, which have been shown to increase feelings of vitality and growth. Although leaders can play a valuable role highlighting meaningful employee work, research shows customers are even more effective at igniting thriving by serving as proof of the impact of their work. For instance, patients who benefitted from Medtronic's health-care devices visit the organization's quarterly meetings to share their appreciation (see Grant, "Outsource Inspiration," this volume). Seeing how their role contributes to the greater whole, employees are energized. When employees have access to more information about where the organization is going in the future and about business plans or strategy, competitors, and industry, they develop stronger feelings of thriving in their work. The new knowledge energizes employees with a sense that they are learning, growing, and developing.

Practice 2: Providing Decision-Making Discretion

Employees are more likely to thrive when empowered to make decisions that affect their work. This sense of autonomy at work fuels vitality and growth. Decision making works in conjunction with broad information sharing. At Alaska Airlines' road show, where the top leadership team visited sites sharing their company's strategy and mission, employees developed their empowerment toolkit. Armed with greater understanding of the big picture, employees were granted control over *how* to achieve company goals, such as resolving customer issues in a proactive and timely manner. This practice is consistent with principles of high-involvement management, where employees have a voice in the workings of the organization and are signaled that they are valuable to the organization. Providing discretion not only sparks energy when employees feel valued for their ideas, but also taps into learning because employees are not told what to do and how to do it. Instead, they are encouraged to figure out the best way to get the job done. The challenge comes when empowerment leads to mistakes. Rather than pull back on empowerment after a mistake, the leader must look for the learning in the experience to garner thriving. This is crucial, as it is very difficult to take initiative when feeling threatened. A leader who frames mistakes as knowledge to be used for learning and improvement will promote thriving and build a more trusting, safe environment for employees to experiment, take risks, and innovate.

Practice 3: Minimizing Incivility

Incivility, such as rude and disrespectful behaviors of co-workers or customers who put others down or demean people for mistakes, impedes thriving. Not tolerating incivility builds feelings of belongingness, which have been shown to increase feelings of vitality and growth. Those who experience incivility find their energy quickly depleted. Fear and anger, often engendered by the experience of incivility, also stops the learning process because negative emotions constrain cognitions and behaviors. In contrast, trust and connectivity create a nurturing environment that enables thriving. Leaders need to set norms about what behaviors are acceptable and call out uncivil behaviors. Danny Meyers, owner of twenty-seven New York City–based restaurants, preaches civility and tolerates nothing less. Bad behavior, even from an exceptional chef, must be corrected quickly. If not, the chef will be gone. Meyers is convinced customers can *taste* incivility.[17] Our research shows that incivility not only hurts employees, but also influences customers and their willingness to do business with your organization. Businesses we have analyzed have learned the hard way that it simply does not pay to harbor uncivil employees, even if they are rainmakers or star performers.[18]

Practice 4: Offering Performance Feedback

Feedback—especially two-way, open, frequent, and guided communication—creates opportunities for learning. This practice builds feelings of competence and, in turn, thriving because feedback helps people know where they stand in terms of their skills, competencies, and performance. Positive feedback energizes employees to seek their full potential. Even constructive feedback, when provided in a supportive way (rather than one that beckons feelings of incivility), garners an interest in learning how to improve. The best organizations encourage employees to seek out feedback rather than to wait for it.[19]

Putting It All Together

Thriving at work can come in many forms, and they are all important. You can enable your own thriving as an individual and also empower others as a leader. This chapter provides a definition of thriving at work and why it is important. It also describes what you can do as an individual and as a leader to enable more thriving at work. Thriving individuals not only have more positive individual outcomes, but they also help their organizations better achieve their goals. Individuals can change their own behavior to craft more meaning, seek out learning opportunities, invest in high-quality connections, and manage energy. But the most impactful seed is to craft organizational practices building autonomy, competence, and belongingness. These practices include providing decision-making discretion, sharing information broadly, minimizing incidents of incivility, and offering performance feedback. We encourage you to begin or to strengthen your journey to build a thriving organization.

A COMPANY THAT EPITOMIZES THRIVING

Zingerman's Community of Businesses

Zingerman's, a world-famous community of businesses in Ann Arbor, Michigan, enables employee thriving at work. Founders Ari Weinzweig and Paul Saginaw had a vision to make a positive difference to customers and the community, but also build a great place to work. They crafted a wide range of strategies, even going so far as to create their own training company, to hold them accountable for living out their mission. A visit to any Zingerman's business clearly shows employees are thriving at work. This living policy of employee thriving has served all well. Zingerman's revenue has been growing, achieving $45 million in 2012.[20] The company's leaders credit the thriving environment they have created as a key factor in their success.

Organizational Practices That Enable Thriving

Wayne Baker has written several cases on Zingerman's. In this sidebar we highlight some of the practices that contribute to their success. *Infor-*

mation is shared. Weinzweig and Saginaw adopted the principles of open-book management. They hold regular "huddles," which are weekly gatherings around a whiteboard at which teams track results. They "keep score" and forecast the next week's numbers. Not only do the team members track financial performance, but they also keep a pulse on service, food quality, and check averages. They also track "fun," which could mean anything from weekly contests to raise customer satisfaction or generate employees' ideas for innovation. This information transparency helps motivate employees to continually improve.

Armed with this information, Weinzweig and Saginaw believe employees will make better decisions. Zingerman's provides employees with *decision-making discretion*. They are encouraged to share ideas with top leaders and are expected to be proactive in interactions with customers, especially in the rare need for service recovery. Zingerman's is structured to be a flexible hierarchy, allowing employees to learn and to grow continually.

Another core value is to minimize episodes of incivility, stressing that leaders need to treat employees in the same way they expect customers to be treated. Employing principles of servant leadership, they have built a civil environment where leaders set the tone and serve as role models. Managers are taught how to deal with employee issues so that conflict is resolved. At the end of each meeting, managers and others take time to express appreciation to employees. Employees are encouraged to keep their own pulse and their group's energy by doing regular energy assessments.

Finally, Zingerman's *provides feedback* to enable employee thriving. Examples include open-book management and the creation of various "mini games," which are short-term incentive plans involving goals, scorecards, and rewards to fix a problem or capitalize on an opportunity. For example, Zingerman's Roadhouse created the "greeter game" to track how long it takes for customers to be welcomed. Other Zingerman's businesses started similar games to improve delivery time, reduce knife injuries in the bakery (which would lower insurance costs), and keep kitchens cleaner. These games help to highlight issues and motivate employees to improve scores. Overall, they have increased frontline employees' learning and energy.

TWEETS

Thriving matters because people feel like they are energized and growing at the same time. It helps people stay at the edge of their game.

To enable thriving at work, encourage employees to cocreate the work environments to be more meaningful and more healthy by building positive relationships.

Leaders can create a more thriving work environment by sharing decision making, information, and feedback throughout the organization.

5

Cultivate Positive Identities

Laura Morgan Roberts

We spend a great deal of time doing "identity work" in organizations. As we introduce and explain ourselves during job interviews, meetings with clients, networking functions, public presentations, and team-building activities, we confront identity questions that are central to our work roles, relationships, and outcomes. Identity questions ask, *Who am I? Who are we? How might our identities impact our capability to work together?* Positive leadership involves shaping, building, and sustaining positive identities for organizational leaders, members, and the organization itself. Leaders are able to unleash resources through the way in which they construct who they are as leaders and also how they help others construct positive identities.

Individuals and groups use images, stories, and descriptions of their key characteristics to define their identities. For example, individuals may define themselves in terms of their physical features, education, friendships, employer, title, accomplishments, and failures. Identities help to explain how an individual or a group relates to other individuals and groups, highlighting differences, similarities, and power/status dynamics.

Most individuals seek to hold positive self-views, desiring to be viewed positively by others. Positive identity construction is the process of (re)defining a person's identity using images, stories, and descriptions that are considered to be positive or valuable in some way. My colleagues, Jane Dutton, Jeff Bednar, and I developed the GIVE model of positive identity to explain four of the most common ways a person might respond positively to the question "Who are you?" at work.[1]

- "I am Growing." I am becoming more like my desired self, by evolving and adapting in positive ways at work. For example, as leaders become more comfortable in their roles and more capable of influencing, mobilizing, and organizing others, they grow closer to their desired leader identities.[2]
- "I am Integrated." The different parts of my identity, such as work roles, demographic characteristics, family status and relationships, educational background, hobbies and interests, domains of expertise, organizational membership, and departmental affiliations are connected in compatible or enriching ways. For example, Education Pioneers, a nonprofit organization, provides business, law, education, and policy leaders with opportunities to integrate their professional backgrounds with their passion for educational reform.
- "I am Virtuous." I possess virtuous qualities such as courage, wisdom, integrity, humility, and compassion, and I display these virtues at work. For example, employees who donate to their company's employee support program are more likely to see themselves and the organization as caring, benevolent, and helpful.[3]
- "I am Esteemed." I am worthy of positive regard; I feel positively about my defining characteristics and group affiliations, and I feel others understand and appreciate my

authentic self at work. For example, employees who partici-
pate in company-sponsored community outreach initiatives
feel better about themselves and about their company. They
define the company as more cooperative, socially responsible, and innovative.[4]

Why Care about Positive Identities?

Positive identity construction unlocks valuable psychological
and social resources in work organizations. When people see
themselves growing at work, by becoming more capable in their
jobs or by becoming better people as a consequence of their
work, they are more likely to experience positive emotions and
to persist through adversity.[5] When people draw upon or integrate different parts of their identities, they are more creative in
generating new ideas and solving problems.[6] For example, this
logic is one of the reasons that IBM has engaged its Employee
Resource groups to draw upon cultural insights of diverse
groups—such as working mothers; visually impaired workers; lesbian, gay, bisexual, and transgender (LGBT) workers;
and Latino/as—to discover new business strategies and work
processes.[7]

People who construct more positive identities are also better
able to cope with threats to their identities, such as being critici-
zed harshly or demeaned at work.[8] Consider hospital cleaners,
who often experience devaluation at work because of their low
professional status, relative to doctors, nurses, and administra-
tors. They are also judged by their "dirty work" responsibilities,
which society generally views as undesirable. Candice Billups,
a hospital cleaner in a cancer unit, constructed a positive, virtuous self-identity as healer and care provider for patients and their
families. She was motivated at work to engage in additional

helping behaviors and to experience increased personal satisfaction, enjoyment, and meaningfulness.[9]

Positive identity construction also generates more diverse, high-quality relationships at work, which are important resources for individuals and organizations. When people focus on character strengths and virtues, and behave virtuously, they are more likely to build trust and respect. People who integrate different parts of themselves, such as previous work roles, domains of expertise, cultural heritage, hobbies, and interests, into their work lives are more likely to build and to sustain a strong network of contacts from these various parts of their lives. This diverse network can help them to leverage opportunities and access resources, benefitting their careers and organizations.[10] These people may also strengthen their relationships with coworkers because they feel more fully known, understood, and appreciated for the distinctive and valued aspects of their work and nonwork lives.

Strategies for Cultivating Positive Identities at Work

According to the GIVE model, a leader can increase the positivity of their identity by defining themselves as Growing, Integrated, Virtuous, and Esteemed. However, the positivity of leaders' identities depends upon their self-views *and the perceptions that others have of them as leaders*.[11] Leaders' identities are more powerful and sustainable when they are validated by followers' perceptions. For instance, leaders who view themselves favorably but behave in an autocratic and narcissistic manner will likely be negatively viewed by subordinates. Ultimately, the positivity of the leader's identity will be contested and the leader's sense of esteem may be threatened. On the

other hand, leaders who practice compassion are more likely
to gain the admiration of followers, reinforcing the positivity
of their virtuous and esteemed selves. In another example,
when leaders display humility, they model how to grow. They
acknowledge their own imperfections, creating a safer culture
in which people can express their feelings of uncertainty and
commit to shared learning and improvement.[12] Thus, leaders
should conscientiously use the following three positive identity
infusions as recommended strategies for positive identity construction. Positive self-views should be reinforced by behaviors
that are consistent with the leader's positive identity claims.

Positive Identity Infusion 1: Use Positive Identity Labels

Identity labels are powerful. When people take on positive
identity labels, they are more likely to engage in desirable behavior.[13] Popular leadership theories use several positive identity labels to define leaders in terms of character strengths and
virtues (e.g., servant leaders, authentic leaders, ethical leaders).
Yet, many leaders are unaware of their own character strengths
and virtues. The Values in Action (VIA) inventory is a useful tool for identifying your top five character strengths and
virtues.[14] Completing this inventory can help leaders to take on
more positive (virtuous) identity labels, which can lead to more
desirable behavior. Finding new ways to use one's top character strengths and virtues at work can also reinforce the positive
identity.[15]

Positive Identity Infusion 2: Design a Developmental Agenda and Monitor Your Growth

The growing self reflects a person's sense of becoming more
like the desired self at work. In the first phase, leaders cultivate

their growing self by building bridges between their past, present, and future. To examine their growth, leaders can use the Leadership Lifeline exercise to map key developmental milestones that have helped them become a leader and the person that they are. These developmental milestones include challenges, disappointments, accomplishments, opportunities, and changes in life status (e.g., marriage, relocation, parenthood). By reflecting on one's leadership lifeline, a leader can deepen understanding of the events that contributed to growth and how things changed over time.

The second phase of cultivating the growing self involves designing a plan for future growth. First, you need to create a developmental agenda by identifying a range of desired possible selves. Ask yourself, who do you think you are capable of becoming in the future? This exercise of envisioning best possible selves and best possible futures has been shown to increase life satisfaction and optimism.[16] Second, continue the development process by finding role models who display the characteristics of these desired possible selves, namely, those who exhibit the positive identities you hope to develop. Third, experiment with your desired possible selves by "trying on" the various identities, imitating the role models you have selected. Fourth, evaluate which of the possible selves you have tried on is the best "fit" for your personality, values, and style. Professionals who are promoted to leadership positions, like investment bankers and consultants, use this four-step process of experimenting with possible selves to effectively adapt to the expectations of their new roles.[17] Leaders can also create their own developmental agendas for addressing shortcomings, building on strengths, and adapting to new roles or assignments, and systematically track their progress toward their established goals.

Positive Identity Infusion 3: Facilitate Reflected Best-Self Engagement

Leadership involves more than constructing more positive identities for leaders—it involves actively helping all members of organizations to construct more positive identities for themselves. Leaders can help themselves and others construct more positive identities at work by discovering and engaging their reflected best selves: visions of who they are, what they do, and when they are at their best. These visions vary from person to person, based upon the person's unique character strengths, talents, competencies, and impact upon others. At their best, people actively engage these valuable qualities and characteristics in ways that promote their own vitality (i.e., increase their feeling of being alive and vibrant) *and* create value for the broader social system (i.e., make significant contributions to people and institutions beyond themselves). Most people have a vague or limited understanding of their best self. They are not aware of their strengths, and they do not know how to engage their strengths most effectively to promote vitality and value creation.

Leaders can use the Reflected Best-Self Exercise™ (RBSE) to help people learn about their character strengths and virtues, talents, and contributions.[18] The RBSE gathers strength-based feedback in the form of contribution stories from professional contacts, such as teachers, coaches, and bosses, and from personal contacts, such as friends and family. Participants review their contribution stories, identify common themes, and develop a written or visual portrait capturing how they make significant contributions when at their best. After completing the RBSE, people can then begin the process of bringing their best self to work more often, by increasing alignment between their work tasks and relationships, and their strengths. Amy Wrzesniewski's chapter in this book, "Engage in Job Crafting," offers several ways to derive deeper meaning from work that may help to promote best-self engagement.

The RBSE can help to build up the Growing Self, the Virtuous Self, the Integrated Self, and the Esteemed Self. Leaders can use best-self feedback to help employees chart new pathways for being at their best more often, and making one's best self even better by expanding one's developmental agenda. The RBSE helps people identify their character strengths and understand why they are so impactful. It also helps people see how their strengths are expressed in different parts of their life. As people realize the similarities in their contribution stories from various counterparts, they begin to build bridges between their multiple identities, such as work- and nonwork-related roles, relationships, and affiliations. In addition, as a vehicle for structured, evidence-based affirmation, the RBSE helps remind people why they are valued and appreciated and inspires them to continue to grow in their areas of strength.[19]

Putting It All Together

Best-selling authors and leadership development experts Dale Carnegie and John Maxwell likened the process of developing people to mining for gold: you must move tons of dirt in the process, but you go in looking for the gold, not the dirt.[20] The more positive characteristics you seek, the more you will find. As leaders use positive identity infusions, they enhance their own and others' sense of self as Growing, Integrated, Virtuous, and Esteemed. Leaders can use positive identity infusions to bring out the best in themselves, and by consequence, bring out the best in others.

TRAGEDY AVERTED

On August 22, 2013, Michael Brandon Hill entered the Ronald E. McNair Discovery Learning Academy in Decatur, Georgia, just outside of Atlanta, armed with an AK-47 and over five hundred rounds of ammunition. He fired one round into the floor. While teachers, staff, and police safely ushered children out of the building, Antoinette Tuff, the school's bookkeeper, engaged the gunman in conversation in the front office.[21] Tuff was not armed with a weapon, but she had at her disposal a very powerful tool: positive identity construction. Hill confessed he felt isolated, unworthy, and despised. In this moment of crisis, Tuff did not disparage him or cower in fear. Instead, she countered each of his negative identity claims with positive identity claims. She connected with the gunman, telling him he was not alone in his pain because, "We all go through something in life" and "I'm sitting with you and talking to you about it right now." And she planted seeds of hope for healing by using her own story, saying, "I tried to commit suicide last year after my husband left me; but look at me now. I'm still working and everything is OK." Through her twenty-minute exchange with this gunman, Tuff facilitated his peaceful surrender, preventing injury and loss of life. Tuff told him that in spite of the threat he had posed, his surrender was honorable: "It's going to be all right, sweetie. I want you to know I love you, OK? I'm proud of you. That's a good thing you're giving up and don't worry about it." Tuff's masterful identity work was heralded in the news media following the incident, the audio recording of her dialogue with the gunman and 911 emergency response went viral on the Internet,[22] and she received a personal phone call from President Obama to recognize her courageous leadership. This life-or-death crisis situation may seem far removed from the leadership realm in which most people typically operate. Yet, the power of positive identity construction is no less significant in everyday organizational life. When leaders cultivate positive identities for themselves and others, they unlock critical psychological and social resources that strengthen individuals and organizations. Thus, positive identity construction lies at the heart of leadership itself.

TWEETS

Positive leadership unlocks valuable resources through shaping, building, and sustaining positive identities.

Who are you at your best? Leaders construct more positive identities at work by discovering and engaging reflected best selves.

Dig for gold in leadership and human development: the more positive characteristics you seek, the more you will find.

6

Engage in Job Crafting

Amy Wrzesniewski

The chances are good that at some point, you have changed an aspect of your job so that it better suited you. Whether you took a different approach to a task you were responsible for, changed an interaction pattern, or refined how you thought about the job in a more general sense, you were engaged in crafting your job. Job crafting is defined as "the physical and cognitive changes individuals make in the task or relational boundaries of their work" and encompasses a vast range of bottom-up moves made by employees to create a more optimal design of their jobs.[1] For example, job crafting occurs when a marketing manager decides to bring her passion for social media into the design of a product launch.[2] It also occurs when an executive takes responsibility for understanding the life *and* work goals of his team and helping them to reach these goals.[3] This chapter explores the benefits of job crafting for employees and their organizations and suggests ways that leaders can support job-crafting efforts.

The Value of Job Crafting

At first blush, job crafting may appear to be an activity that *should* make organizational leaders nervous. The thought of employees taking liberties with the design of their jobs to create changes that better meet employee needs could inspire fear in the hearts of those tasked with managing such employees. However, whether organizational leaders realize it or not, job crafting is widespread; employees from a range of industries and sectors and from the executive leadership of their organizations to the entry level engage in it.[4]

Given the ubiquitous nature of job crafting, it should come as good news to learn that a growing body of research has documented a range of benefits—to employees *and* to organizations—of job crafting. First, job crafting allows employees to change the meaning of their work in ways that suit them, setting the stage for their work to be more meaningful.[5] Second, job crafting relies on a treasured organizational resource: employee proactivity.[6] The changes employees make to their jobs allow them to more optimally bridge the demands of their jobs and the resources they have to meet them.[7] Third, employees who engage in job crafting, whether individually or in collaboration with others on their team, perform significantly better than those who do not.[8] Fourth, job crafters are more engaged in their work and are less likely to be absent from their jobs.[9] Fifth, employees who craft their jobs become happier employees in the eyes of their coworkers and managers;[10] they report more positive emotions[11] and better mental health and well-being.[12] In all, the evidence supports job crafting as an activity that benefits both the employee and the organization.

How does job crafting lead to these benefits? By customizing the design of their own jobs, employees are able to meet their needs for control over their work, develop a positive self-image on the job, and establish a connection to others in the workplace. Through these pathways, needs are met, and employee well-being results. This improved well-being matters for employee effectiveness at work. Indeed, it is the increased happiness shown by job crafters that leads to the boost in their work performance.[13] Through taking charge of their own work and altering it in ways that better meet their needs, employees foster well-being, which is good for them and for their organizations.

Strategies for Crafting a Job

How, then, can employees engage in job crafting? Whether your focus is crafting your own job or supporting those you manage in crafting theirs, there are four strategies that can help spark job crafting and its individual and organizational benefits. Each of these strategies can be undertaken in isolation or in combination, and each is likely to spark a process of bringing proactive change at work that continues over time.

Strategy 1: Optimize the Job You Have

Analyze the job you have as you currently execute it, paying particularly close attention to how you are spending your time in the tasks and interactions that comprise your work. Consider the ways in which this allocation of time and energy may be altered to give you a better chance to engage in the interactions that support needs for control, positive identity, and connection with others. Think about the values you most want to express in your work, the strengths you would enjoy deploying at work, and the passions you want to bring into the work. Employees can be rather creative in their ability to shape the tasks and interactions of their jobs to allow for the expression of more of their values, strengths, and passions at work.[14] Although you continue to meet your responsibilities to the organization for what you are expected to accomplish, you can optimize the design of the job to proactively shape the meaning of the work and who you experience yourself to be on the job. To help you craft your job, see the Job Crafting Exercise, a tool designed by the author and her colleagues, at Jobcrafting.org.

Strategy 2: Re-vision the Relational Landscape of Work

Other people help to give work meaning and shape our experience of what we do each day.[15, 16] Most jobs involve series of interactions—some repeated, some unique—that organize, punctuate, and create the structure of our work. One powerful way to guide job crafting is to think carefully about the quality of the interactions and connections you are having in the course of your work. Identify sites of interdependence that are life-giving and support the meaning you wish to find in your work as well as those that make your work more difficult. Invest in the former and troubleshoot the latter. Do the same with interactions and relationships that occur outside of the interdependent ties that are necessary to execute your work. By simultaneously moving toward those interactions that support the identity and meaning you seek in the job and working to improve, minimize, or circumvent the others, over time you will create a relational landscape in your job that enables job crafting. Even in jobs that by design do not involve much interaction, it is possible to seek out ways to connect with others through what you are doing on the job—even if these interactions happen off, or outside, the job. Building a set of interactions and relationships that support the meaning and identity you seek in your work also creates resources for altering the tasks that comprise your job. Investing in more difficult sites of interdependence to learn why the tie is less than optimal can be pivotal in transforming it. If such investments of time and energy are unproductive, limiting contact or changing the mode of contact, if possible, may help to blunt the negative impact of the relationship and leave more energy for promising interactions with others. By proactively and thoughtfully building ties with others, you can create opportunities to learn important skills or to receive needed support that will enable you to take on new tasks or to take a different approach to existing ones.[17]

Strategy 3: Queue It Up

One of the less radical job-crafting moves you can readily make in your work is to reorder the tasks and interactions that comprise your day. Reflect on the tasks that are sources of engagement, energy, and enjoyment in the work. Do the same for the interactions and relationships you have in your job. Think about what and where your discretion lies in exercising control over when these tasks and interactions occur. For some, this might mean starting the day by "taking your medicine" and getting through the least engaging and meaningful tasks and interactions, so that after this work has been tended, the more engaging and meaningful parts fill the rest of the day. The temporal ordering of work is adjusted to feed a sense of growing momentum, meaning, and enjoyment as the day goes on. The reverse strategy is also effective: by engaging in a task or interaction that is engaging and meaningful, resources are created that can make executing a less desired task or interaction more palatable and less of a drain.[18]

Strategy 4: Aspirational Job Crafting

The previous three strategies focus on bringing alignment between the employee and the job so that the task, relational, and cognitive boundaries of work are bent in service of a realization of meaning and expression of identity that is more ideal.[19] However, it is also possible to craft a job toward a future aspirational reality that does not currently exist in the job or organization. Although more ambitious—and potentially riskier—than job crafting that hews more closely to the job as designed, aspirational job crafting can beget more pronounced changes in well-being and effectiveness through the nature and size of the changes it promotes.[20] Aspirational job crafters focus their efforts on experiences of meaning in the work or expressions of their identity that do not yet exist in the work and look for ways to move their work in that direction over time. For example, a corporate writer who imagines becoming a key public face of the corporation can begin to create opportunities to manage communications in the media on an ad hoc basis, slowly building trust to manage more frequent written and live presentations of the firm. In doing so, the writer crafts an identity that reflects a broader range and use of communications media and derives meaning from the work that reflects these changes.

Designing Organizations for Job Crafting

The previous section focuses on strategies that employees (and organization leaders) can use to craft their jobs. This section presents a set of moves that organization leaders and managers can make to facilitate employee job crafting and to help align the changes employees make to their jobs with the general strategic direction of the organization. Although job crafting is inherently an individual activity—employees cannot easily be required to craft their jobs—managers and leaders are the "architects of the contexts" in which crafting is enabled, or not. Though job crafting often occurs beneath the radar of managers and leaders, they have at least four key ways in which to encourage and enable job crafting to flourish in their organizations.

Boost Autonomy and Support

Job crafting depends in part on the opportunities employees perceive for taking some liberties with the task, relational, and cognitive boundaries of their jobs. When employees sense that they have autonomy in how they execute their work, they are more likely to engage in job crafting. By emphasizing the ends for which employees are responsible while loosening up the management of the means where possible, managers and leaders increase the likelihood that employees will craft their jobs. This move also communicates a powerful signal that employees can be trusted to reach the desired end points, which itself constitutes a form of support for job crafting. Managers and leaders can offer more active forms of support as well, such as facilitating the removal of barriers to job crafting for employees where appropriate.

Build Job Crafting into Developmental Plans

Effective, supportive leaders understand that employees are working to develop themselves while they work to achieve the aims of the organization. Through job crafting, employees take control of shaping key parts of the meaning and identity that they experience in their work, changing the boundaries of their jobs in ways that allow for personal growth and well-being.[21]

In developmental meetings in which employees chart their goals for the next quarter or year, managers can ask about the changes employees might wish to make to the design of their jobs, supporting them in making these changes where possible and appropriate. Such a practice sends a strong signal of support to employees, endowing them with a sense that proactivity and initiative are accepted and celebrated by their employer. An even more supportive step would involve managers and leaders offering opportunities for additional training and education in order to pursue job-crafting goals. Recent research has suggested that crafting a job in this way can lead to promotions and moves to other roles—both developmental outcomes that managers and leaders could benefit from as employees grow their careers within the organization.

Communicate Strategic Goals

Employees' job-crafting efforts could be powerfully affected by having a deep understanding of the strategic goals and direction of the organization. For example, in a classic case, when former CEO Paul Allaire of Xerox articulated that return on assets would be a primary focus going forward, a newly hired John Clendenin began to craft his job to focus his tasks on logistic supply-chain improvements that would allow him to have the impact that he desired while meeting important strategic goals.[22] When employees have a strong sense of what the organization and its leadership are trying to achieve and why, they are in a better position to potentially align their job-crafting efforts with where the organization is heading.

Hold Job-Crafting Swap Meets

Research has shown that collaborative job crafting yields positive outcomes for employees and organizations.[23] One natural opportunity that arises from job crafting occurs when an employee wishes to scale back on a certain task or relationship to free up time and space to cultivate or invest in another. For interdependent work, or even when the task in question is a nonnegotiable one that must be executed, it may be possible to swap a task with a coworker. At a group level, it could be productive for employees on the same team to engage in the Job Crafting Exercise to map their ideal job-crafting moves, sharing their plans and discovering opportunities for task and relationship exchanges that leave each employee closer to crafting a more ideal job. At Google, efforts to identify group-level job-crafting opportunities have helped focus work teams on where such swaps would be possible and optimally productive and satisfying for Googlers.

Putting It All Together

Job crafting, or the practice of changing the task, relational, and/or cognitive boundaries of a job, represents a powerful practice that employees engage in to shape the meaning of their work and their identities on the job. Employees stand to gain a more positive experience of their work and increased well-being while organizations benefit from employees' gains in performance and decreased absenteeism.[24] Through employing strategies ranging from the simple queuing of work tasks and interactions to the more sweeping possibilities captured by aspirational job crafting, employees can take concrete steps to craft their jobs. Occupying the middle ground are strategies that help employees to optimize the jobs they have and to re-vision the relational landscape of their work. Though any of these strategies are likely to help employees in their job-crafting efforts, the context that managers and leaders can build to support job crafting at the organizational level can multiply the power of these individual-level moves. Whether by supporting individual employee efforts to job craft or building contexts in which teams of employees can engage in job crafting at the group level, managers and leaders occupy a unique position from which to support employees as they develop themselves through their work and, in the process, their organizations.

CREATING SPACE AND SUPPORT FOR JOB CRAFTING AT BURT'S BEES

Founded in a one-room schoolhouse in 1984 by Roxanne Quimby and Burt Shavitz, Burt's Bees has grown to become a national force in environmentally friendly personal products. In their compelling case study of job crafting at Burt's Bees, Jane E. Dutton and Justin M. Berg describe the job-crafting practices of four employees in jobs that range greatly in their complexity and discretion.[25]

One key theme across employees highlighted in the case is the support offered by management for the job-crafting efforts of Burt's Bees' employees. For example, Andy, a maintenance technician with a deep passion for the process improvements that would normally be the province of company engineers, saw an opportunity to collect data on ways in which certain manufacturing processes could be improved and made more efficient. He approached management to win their support as he conducted experiments to determine which processes were most efficient. Though not formally part of his maintenance technician job, with the support of management, the experiments were conducted and the results had an impact on processes at Burt's Bees.

Similarly, Mindy, a customer care representative, regularly involves her manager in her efforts to seek out new challenges and tasks that need to be done for the good of the organization. Mindy uses job crafting to break up the monotony in her work, involving herself where needed by her manager and learning new skills in the process. For both Andy and Mindy, the support of management in their efforts to transcend the boundaries of their prescribed jobs is key in their ability to successfully craft their jobs and remain maximally engaged in and excited about their work.

A third example described in the casework involves Jake, a compounding department employee responsible for mixing ingredients to create products for Burt's Bees. Jake's passion for understanding new machines and how they are assembled led him to reach out and engage in relational job crafting with the assembly group by getting involved with and learning about what they do. In Jake's description, this group was initially suspicious of his curiosity about their work, and it was managers who facilitated the tie between Jake and this other group of employees.

By helping an employee overcome relational barriers to job crafting, management at Burt's Bees directly supports the relational job-crafting efforts of their members. The openness to and support of job crafting among employees from a wide range of departments and levels helps to ensure that employees feel supported and empowered to move beyond the boundaries of their jobs for their own—and the organization's—benefit.

TWEETS

Craft your job: making small changes boosts happiness and effectiveness.

Optimizing the job you have can be as simple as interacting with the people who boost the meaning of your work.

The job you have is just a starting point: change the design and the flow of your tasks and interactions to discover deeper meaning at work.

III

TAP INTO THE GOOD

As a positive leader, possibilities abound for increasing individual and organizational capacities for excellence by tapping into the good. This section unpacks this aspirational goal by offering three distinctive approaches on what tapping into the good means. The first focuses on individual and organizational practices that promote virtuousness, namely, behaviors that represent the best of the human condition such as gratitude, compassion, honesty, and love. A second approach directs attention to how you and other leaders serve as role models, helping to create an ethical culture even when circumstances are working against you. The third approach encourages you and other positive leaders to articulate and to pursue a higher purpose. A higher purpose involves going beyond the normal focus on profits to create a more aspirational vision that embraces and fosters actions that serve the collective good. This section reveals practices that call forth moral goodness in people and in the organization, which is valuable on its own as well as useful in fostering desirable outcomes (such as higher performance, greater engagement, and more authentic actions).

7

Activate Virtuousness

Kim Cameron

Consider two different business organizations. One is characterized by a single-minded focus on creating profitability and shareholder value as key indicators of success. Competition, productivity, carrot-and-stick incentives, and high pressure for performance characterize the culture. This organization frequently leads employees to demonstrate selfishness, manipulation, secrecy, and distrust of their colleagues.

Another business organization is characterized by a focus on creating abundance and human well-being as key indicators of success. The work culture emphasizes appreciation, collaboration, positive energy, and meaningfulness. This organization produces social relationships typified by compassion, loyalty, trustworthiness, respect, and forgiveness.

The first business is common and one with which we are all familiar. The second is less common, but describes more closely what we mean by a virtuous organization. These organizations help members achieve their very best and reach extraordinarily positive outcomes. They implement universally valued ennobling attributes, such as forgiveness, gratitude, honesty, compassion, and love. When organizations engender these characteristics, they are labeled as virtuous.

The Value of Virtuousness

Organizations do not need to trade a desire for financial success for virtuous practices. An extensive amount of evidence shows that demonstrations of virtuousness in work organizations are associated with desirable outcomes, including profitability.

Virtuousness is not merely saccharine, smiley-faced behavior. Rather, it has a tangible impact on both individuals at work and their organizations. Gratitude, forgiveness, transcendence, compassion, honesty, hope, and love are among the virtues found to predict desired outcomes in people.[1] Increased commitment, satisfaction, motivation, positive emotions, effort, physical health, and psychological health are among the outcomes produced. Evidence even suggests that heart rhythms, brain functioning, physiological alignments, nervous system health, memory, and brain cortex thickness are positively affected by virtuousness.[2] When people behave virtuously, positive results occur physiologically, emotionally, intellectually, and socially.

The irony associated with virtuousness is that, by definition, virtues are of inherent worth. Virtuousness is its own reward and the preeminent condition to which people aspire. Achieving a payoff or some other benefit is unnecessary for making virtuousness relevant and valuable.

On the other hand, if observable bottom-line results are not detected in organizations, attention to virtuousness usually becomes subservient to the very real pressures of enhancing financial return and organizational benefit.[3] Few leaders invest in practices or processes that do not produce profitability, productivity, and customer satisfaction. Without a visible payoff, those with stewardship for organizational resources tend to ignore virtuousness and consider it of little relevance to important stakeholders. Finding an association between virtuousness and desired organizational outcomes is important because it causes leaders to pay attention.

Evidence of Virtuousness and Performance in Organizations

Empirical evidence shows when virtuousness scores improve, important organizational outcomes also increase. In particular, significant improvements have been found in profitability, productivity, quality, innovation, customer loyalty, and employee engagement.[4] Examples of the virtues assessed in these studies include gratitude, forgiveness, compassion, trustworthiness, integrity, and transcendence. Even in organizations that recently downsized and faced the prospect of common occurrences,[5] such as low morale, scapegoating of leaders, diminished trust, and politicized environments, performance increased markedly over time when virtuous practices were implemented as a part of the downsizing activities.[6] These results were observed subsequent to improvements in virtuousness scores, so causal directionality can be inferred in these studies.[7] In the U.S. airline and financial services industries, virtuous practices were also found to be highly predictive of financial performance over subsequent years, even though these publicly traded firms were under constant pressure to return value to shareholders.[8] A conclusion drawn from these studies is that financial performance follows virtuousness in organizations. People and organizations do better when virtuousness is demonstrated.

Enabling Virtuousness

How, then, is virtuousness fostered in organizations? What are examples of practices that can be implemented? This section describes three such practices.

Expressing Gratitude

One of the easiest virtues to implement is the expression of gratitude. Frequent and sincere expressions of appreciation have been found to produce dramatic effects on individuals and organizations. In one study, college students were assigned to keep a daily or weekly journal. Some were to record events for which they were grateful, some focused on neutral events, and others on problem occurrences. Students who kept gratitude journals experienced better physical health, better social relationships, and better cognitive performance than the other students.[9]

In a study of thirty health-care organizations, frequent expressions of gratitude and periodic gratitude visits to other employees were the second-highest predictor of improvement in outcomes such as quality of care, patient satisfaction, employee engagement, and turnover.[10]

Some practical hints for fostering gratitude in organizations include the following:

- **Journal.** Encourage employees (or family members) to keep a gratitude journal. Have them keep track each day of at least three things that occurred for which they are grateful.
- **Cards.** Distribute three gratitude cards each day. Write a short expression of thanks to at least three people in your organization each day.

- **Meetings.** Begin each meeting by asking participants to share one thing that occurred during the week for which they are grateful. Or, end each meeting with the same activity so that people leave with positive energy.
- **Positively embarrass.** Positively embarrass someone each day, by verbally complimenting or expressing gratitude to a person in the presence of another person who cares.
- **Comparisons.** Take stock each day of your privileges and gifts. Compare your circumstances to those of others around you who may be struggling. Count your blessings.[11]

Enabling Forgiveness

Harm, trauma, and injustice are common occurrences in organizations. They frequently lead to retribution, condemnation, victimization, and revenge. As a result, individual and organizational performance almost always deteriorates. The challenge facing leaders is to help organizations heal, replenish, restore positive energy, and enhance resiliency. Enabling forgiveness is one of the most effective mechanisms for achieving these outcomes. Empirical research indicates that institutionalizing forgiveness in organizations is among the most powerful predictors of improvement in productivity, employee satisfaction, decreased turnover, innovation, quality, and profitability.[12] Organizations with a forgiving culture experience more trusting alliances, social capital, workplace humaneness, customer care, and a sense of calling among employees.[13]

Forgiveness does not appear in isolation. It always occurs in collaboration with other virtues such as compassion, caring, and love. Forgiveness does not require abandoning anger or resentment. One can be angry yet forgive, and one can forgive without pardoning, minimizing, or dismissing the offense. Forgiveness is active, not passive, in transforming negative emotions and attitudes into positive ones. It fosters healing, restitution, and restoration in both giver and receiver.

In studies of successful organizations that experienced traumas, ranging from downsizing and job loss to law-breaking and unethical or abusive occurrences, leaders played an important role in fostering forgiveness. The following are some cues for enabling and encouraging forgiveness:

- **Redefinition.** Acknowledge the harm or injustice, as well as the anger and resentment, but define the event as an opportunity to move forward. Identify a new, positive target rather than dwelling on the past wrong.
- **Meaningfulness.** Associate the objectives being pursued with a higher purpose that provides personal meaning for organization members. This higher purpose replaces a focus on self with a focus on an elevated objective.
- **Focus on excellence.** Forgiveness is not synonymous with tolerance of error, excusing mistakes, or lowering expectations. It does not lower the existing standard, so continue to focus on improvement, lessons learned, and excellence.
- **Support.** Provide opportunities for interpersonal interaction and conversation. Forgiveness usually requires opportunities for verbal expressions, empathetic listening, and human support. Humanize the individuals involved. Separate acts from persons. People can forgive others while abhorring their actions.
- **Justice.** Honor fairness and equity. Work toward justice for offenders and restoration for those harmed. Many people have difficulty forgiving when justice, apology, or restitution is absent.

Facilitating Transcendence

Transcendence refers to positive deviance, a sense of profound purpose, and the realization of an ideal. It is one of the universally prescribed virtues from Aristotle, Confucius, and Thomas Aquinas[14] relating to inspiration and elevation—and what leads people to experience awe and wonder.[15] Experiencing a sense of calling in work or in life is an example of transcendence.[16] As with other virtues, experiencing transcendence has been found to produce positive effects in individuals and organizations. Individuals are more cooperative, creative, motivated, have more immunological strength, feel more gratitude, experience greater life satisfaction, and have greater feelings of well-being when they experience transcendence.[17] Commitment, prosocial behavior, teamwork, courtesy, compliance, citizenship, and reciprocity all are significantly associated with transcendence and elevation in organizations.[18]

One tool for fostering transcendence is to develop an "Everest goal," based on the idea that climbing Mt. Everest represents the peak, culmination, or supreme achievement that people can imagine. Everest goals are not just fantasies or dreams. They possess special attributes, making them transcendent in their characteristics.[19]

Everest goals share the attributes of highly effective goal setting, summarized by the commonly used acronym, SMART:

  S = *Specific* versus general. A specific goal provides a clear
     standard or level of performance.
  M = *Measurable* versus vague. A measurable goal can be
     clearly assessed.
  A = *Aligned* versus unrelated. Aligned goals are consistent
     with the purposes of the organization.

$R =$ *Realistic* versus impossible to attain. A realistic goal is
   difficult but not impossible.
$T =$ *Time bound* versus limitless. A time-bound goal is not
   open-ended.

What sets an Everest goal apart, however, are five unique
attributes leading to an experience of transcendence and elevation:

- **Positive deviance.** It aims at extraordinary, spectacular,
  remarkable performance, inspiring a sense of wonder and
  awe. It is virtuous, focusing on achieving the best of the
  human condition, not just mere success.
- **Goods of first intent.** A good of first intent possesses
  inherent value and is desirable because of its intrinsic
  worth. It is inherently virtuous. A good of second intent is
  desirable for the sake of obtaining something else, such as
  profit, prestige, or power. People never tire of goods of first
  intent, but goods of second intent lead to satiation.[20]
- **Possessing an affirmative orientation.** It does not merely
  focus on solving problems, reducing obstacles, overcoming
  challenges, or removing difficulties. Rather, an Everest goal
  also focuses on opportunities and possibilities. It is likely to
  emphasize strengths and potential more than weaknesses
  and obstacles.
- **Representing a contribution.** It focuses on making a contribution rather than merely seeking a personal benefit or
  reward, and on creating value in place of attaining self-
  centered acquisitions. Contribution trumps achievement.
- **Creating and fostering sustainable positive energy.** It is
  inherently energizing and does not require an external

motivator or incentive. People are not exhausted by pursuing an Everest goal but instead are uplifted, elevated, and energized. The goal itself provides the necessary positive energy.

Several examples of organizational Everest goals are Ford, at the turn of the twentieth century, aiming to democratize the auto industry; then, fifty years later, Sony wanting to change the image of Japanese quality; Apple's goal of "one-person, one-computer" in the 1980s; Prudential, at the turn of the twenty-first century, seeking to ensure secure retirement for ten million people; and Interface driving to become a net contributor to a positive carbon footprint. Dramatic success followed in each case.

Putting It All Together

Virtuousness is commonplace in most people's lives and organizations. Most of us frequently experience gratitude, forgiveness, transcendence, kindness, love, and trustworthiness. However, virtuous practices are often shelved when the pressure is on, resources get tight, achieving results is paramount, the competition is gaining, major blunders occur, uncertainty predominates, and disagreements arise. Virtuousness is deemed too soft, too saccharine, and too naive to achieve the needed outcomes. Our research shows just the opposite. Performance increases at all levels when leaders foster virtuousness, organizations implement virtuousness, and individuals demonstrate virtuousness. Activating virtuousness pays.

IMPLEMENTING VIRTUOUS PRACTICES AT GRIFFIN HOSPITAL

At Griffin Hospital, in Derby, Connecticut, the popular vice president of operations, Patrick Charmel, was forced to resign by the board of directors. The employees rebelled and pressured the board of directors to replace the current chief executive officer (CEO) and president with Charmel. Within six months of his return, however, the hospital's decimated financial circumstances necessitated downsizing, and some of the very people who supported Charmel's return lost their jobs. The most likely consequences of downsizing are deteriorating loyalty and morale, perceptions of injustice and duplicity, blaming, accusations, cynicism, and anger. Layoffs and retrenchment almost always lead to deteriorating performance.

Instead, the opposite occurred at Griffin. Upon his return, Charmel made a concerted effort to implement virtuous practices. He institutionalized forgiveness, optimism, loving relationships, and integrity. Throughout the organization, stories of compassion and acts of kindness and virtuousness were almost daily fare. One respondent said, "We are in a very competitive health-care market, so we have differentiated ourselves through our compassionate and caring culture.... I know it sounds trite, but we really do love our patients.... People love working here, and our employees' family members love us too.... Even when we downsized, Pat maintained the highest levels of integrity. He told the truth, and he shared everything. He got the support of everyone by his genuineness and personal concern.... It wasn't hard to forgive."

Specific actions included installing queen-size beds in the maternity ward so fathers could sleep with mothers rather than sit in a chair through the night, creating numerous communal rooms for family gatherings, allowing patients' pets or providing pets for patients, hanging original paintings with virtuous themes on walls, and placing Jacuzzis in the maternity ward.

As a result, Griffin is the only hospital to be listed in Fortune's Top 100 Best Places to Work for ten consecutive years. It is only one of three U.S. hospitals given the Distinction for Leadership and Innovation in Patient-Centered Care Award. Griffin also was designated in the top 5 percent of

Distinguished Hospitals for Clinical Excellence and received the Platinum Innovation Prize. And yes, revenues have soared.

TWEETS

Virtuous practices pay off by producing higher levels of organizational performance as well as more employee flourishing.

When people behave virtuously in organizations, positive results occur physiologically, emotionally, intellectually, and socially.

Especially effective strategies for leaders include expressing gratitude, enabling forgiveness, and facilitating transcendence.

8

Lead an Ethical Organization

David M. Mayer

Consider your own work experience for a moment: Have you ever had a boss that you considered unethical, unfair, rude, or sleazy? Likely most of us have had to deal with the difficulties of working for this type of boss. But equally likely, many bosses have also been people we admire, respect, and view as ethical role models. In this chapter, I focus on what it means to be an ethical leader, why it matters, as well as personal strategies and organizational practices that enable bosses to lead ethically.

What is an ethical leader? We typically describe someone as "ethical" if their behavior is consistent with broader societal values and beliefs regarding desired conduct.[1] Three key aspects of being an ethical leader are (1) role-modeling ethical and appropriate conduct; (2) treating others in a just, caring, and respectful manner; and (3) actively managing the ethical behavior of employees.[2,3] The first two key aspects are reflected in the *moral person* component of ethical leadership, as ethical leaders are fair, trustworthy, and consider their employees' needs a priority. The last key aspect exemplifies the *moral manager* component, as ethical leaders encourage appropriate and desired ethical behavior. They also discourage unethical employee behavior by communicating about ethics and using rewards—and punishments—to encourage ethical conduct.[4] Most people think of the moral person component of ethical leadership when considering leaders who are ethical role models. However, as a leader who wants to influence his/her employees' behavior, the moral manager component is also critical to help lead an ethical organization.[5]

What Is the Value of Being an Ethical Leader?

Do ethical leaders influence their employees' attitudes and behaviors? The answer is a resounding yes.[6] Being an ethical leader is an important end in itself because it is simply the right thing to do to try to live in accordance with one's values. But it also has tangible benefits for both employees and leaders. Research demonstrates that when employees view their leader as ethical, they are more likely to be satisfied with their jobs and report greater commitment to their organization.[7, 8] Employees are also more likely to view their work as important and meaningful.[9] Ethical leaders influence their employees' behavior too. Ethical leaders promote behavior that is desirable, but not required by one's job description, that aims to help others in the organization.[10] Employees who are led by ethical leaders are also less likely to engage in unethical behaviors, ranging from a minor indiscretion such as being late to a serious criminal offense such as stealing large sums of money.[11] Finally, when employees report that their leader is ethical, they actually perform better on the job.[12]

Why are ethical leaders so effective in influencing their employees? One explanation relates to the norm of reciprocity,[13] which governs much of human behavior. It prescribes that when one person is treated well by another, they are obliged to reciprocate with positive behavior. Another explanation is that when employees are led by ethical leaders, they are more likely to identify with their group and organization, subsequently behaving in ways to help the collective.[14] A final explanation is that employees often look to their work environment to determine the appropriate way to behave. Ethical leaders serve as role models, and employees learn how to act in their group or organization.[15, 16] Because ethical leaders engender reciprocity, an increased sense of identity, and serve as models for appropriate conduct, employees are more likely to feel good about their job and act in ways that serve the leader and the organization.

How Can I Improve My Own Ethical Leadership?

The positive benefits provide adequate motivation for leaders to ask: What can I do to help be seen as an ethical leader by others? This section discusses several tried-and-true tactics that may be employed to improve one's reputation as an ethical leader. You may already be using some of these strategies, and others you can add to your repertoire.

Strategy 1: Make Sure to Walk the Talk

Many leaders believe that doing the right thing is important, but talking about ethics or values should be relegated to other life domains such as family or religion. They may believe that employees' values are set by the time they start working at their organization. Although values are important drivers of behavior, ethical leaders play a critical role in raising awareness that certain decisions have an ethical component. For example, an ethical leader may highlight that a decision to do business in a certain country may not be illegal, but adhering to the country's business norms may violate the company's code of conduct. It is critical for leaders to discuss ethics and values, and how the decisions they make fit with the company's espoused values and mission. Talking about ethics is not enough. Ethical leaders must behave in line with their words.[17] When leaders espouse the importance of being ethical, but then promote individuals who are disrespectful or dishonest high performers, it can damage how much the leaders will be trusted in the future.

Strategy 2: Find Your Mantra

Being ethical may seem to be natural, but it takes a lot of work. Much like athletes who need to train, ethical leaders must develop tools to keep their moral compass working at all times.[18] Developing a mantra is a way to keep one's values at the top of one's mind. A few examples of a mantra are the following: What would my children/parents think if they saw me engage in this behavior?; Would I be comfortable if this was on the front page of the *Wall Street Journal*?; What would someone I respect or a religious deity think of my actions? It is useful to have a mantra, as well as other reminders, such as regularly reading an inspirational quote about living a good life, decorating office space with reminders of what matters in life, or keeping a journal to reflect on one's actions.

Strategy 3: Avoid Self-Serving Pitfalls

We have a unique gift for justifying and rationalizing behavior,[19] as we are skilled at interpreting our own actions as not violating ethical principles. It is important to see when we may be falling into these biases. We tend to fall for self-interested reasons, when we really want something such as a promotion, a big account, or meeting performance objectives. When wrestling with an ethical decision, make sure to ask if your ethical decision was aligned with your self-interest. If it is in line with a personally desired outcome, you may consider revisiting your decision, making sure you are doing what is right—and not just what is best for you. For example, your company decides to move and you, as the leader, decide you are entitled to the largest office. Is it fair, given your seniority, or are you considering if you are using "fairness" to justify your own self-interest? To be clear, falling into these pitfalls does not mean you are a bad person. But being vigilant helps you act more in line with your values.

Strategy 4: Do Not Go at It Alone

Becoming an ethical leader is not a solo voyage. Developing high-quality relationships with trusted individuals will give you honest feedback about your behavior. An interesting thing happens as you move up in management—employees will be less likely to critique your behavior. As a result, you tend to get an overly rosy view of your own and the organization's actions.[20] People must be able to tell you when you are not acting in line with your values, and also show pride in you when you do the right thing—especially under difficult circumstances. Having a support group is valuable when you must make difficult ethical decisions. Being an ethical leader is not a solitary road; it should include a community of trusted challengers and advocates.

What Practices Can My Organization Implement to Be More Ethical?

In addition to individual strategies that help you to grow as an ethical leader, it is critical to implement organizational practices creating an ethical environment in your organization.

These practices provide the foundation for building an ethical culture and, ultimately, an ethical organization.

Practice 1: Your Ethics Code Is More Than Window Dressing

Essentially, all companies have a code of conduct. Interestingly, simply having the code does not ensure ethical behavior. Research demonstrates that a code of conduct must be lived through the practices and policies developed by management.[21] Thus leaders should make sure that the ethical code of conduct is a living, breathing document that is regularly implemented in organizational decisions.

Practice 2: Bring in the Right Troops

Individuals tend to be attracted to organizations where they perceive a cultural fit. And organizations tend to hire applicants they perceive to be a fit.[22] This process creates a workforce of similar, like-minded people, which can be good or bad, depending on whether the company has an ethical culture or not. Therefore, emphasis should be placed on hiring employees who are ethical. Although competence is a basic requirement for new hires, so is a desire to do good and to live by the company's mission and values. Finding ethical employees can be achieved by learning about a person's character and values, asking behavioral interview questions, using integrity tests, requiring and vetting references, and understanding the culture of companies the applicant previously worked for.

Practice 3: Do an Ethics Audit

How can you find out if your organization is ethical? Do an ethics audit by surveying employees about the various practices used by the company. These practices can include recruitment, selection, orientation, training, performance management, and compensation. It can be difficult for management to get an accurate sense, especially from the ground floor. So performing an ethics audit is a great way to figure out what practices should remain strong, and which ones should be amended to improve the organization's ethical culture. An important caveat is that employees must be "psychologically safe," feeling free to report their true beliefs and attitudes without fear of negative repercussions.

Practice 4: Remind Employees about a Larger Purpose

For many people, a job is not simply a paycheck, but an opportunity to have a meaningful life.[23] For the millennial generation, making a positive difference in the world holds high value. To connect with employees' desire for fulfillment, organizational leaders need to highlight that employees are not only contributing to financial performance but also having a positive effect on others or their community. Companies can emphasize this higher ambition through the use of employee newsletters, company websites, and awards that demonstrate the exemplary behaviors of employees and celebrate their positive contributions.

Putting It All Together

To develop your ethical leadership capabilities, engage in several strategies, such as walking the talk, finding your mantra, avoiding self-serving pitfalls, and not going at it alone. At an organizational level, an ethical leader must develop several practices, such as ensuring the code of ethics is more than window dressing, hiring the right employees, doing an ethics audit, and reminding employees about a larger purpose. Being an ethical leader takes a lot of effort, but working on these personal strategies and developing practices will help you to lead an ethical organization.

A COMPANY AND CEO THAT EXEMPLIFY ETHICS—KELLY SERVICES AND CARL CAMDEN

Kelly Services, a Fortune 500 company based in Troy, Michigan, has many hallmarks of an ethical organization. It was founded in 1946 by William-Russell Kelly and has emerged as one of the leaders in the staffing industry with over seven thousand employees and annual revenue of over $5 billion. Kelly Services is the world's largest scientific staffing provider, ranking among the leaders in information technology (IT), engineering, and financial staffing. Listed among *Fortune Magazine*'s Most Admired Companies, Kelly Services is often heralded as a beacon of ethical conduct in a competitive industry that is often mired in illegal and unethical behavior.

The CEO and president of Kelly Services, Carl Camden, is a big reason why this company has developed its ethical reputation. He holds a PhD in communications and is a former tenured professor, making him an atypical CEO. Stemming from Camden's leadership, Kelly Services engages in several practices that help to create its ethical organizational culture. The organization has some novel practices, including the following:

Live Your Code of Ethics

At Kelly Services, the code of ethics is more than just window dressing. Kelly Services is a global company, often making important decisions about working with organizations, governments, countries, or cultures with different views about ethics. Kelly Services has clarity on what it stands for, and even when there is money to be made, they turn down contracts forcing them to violate their ethical business approach. As Camden says, employees do not see the code of ethics as "just words on a paper," but something backed by "actual business decisions."

Reward the Good

Many organizations believe they can legislate behavior by creating a lot of rules and punishing those who do not conform. Although rules are important, and punishment is sometimes necessary, Kelly Services takes a different approach. Camden says, "Our goal is to make believers, disciples who aggressively support doing the right thing. I spend more time trying to praise employees who are emitting good than [I spend trying] to prevent them from doing bad." A prestigious award within the company, the William Russell Kelly Award goes to not only high performers but also ethical people who live the Kelly Services values. Camden explains, "The nomination process yields a good number people who are heroes in terms of expressing the belief system as well as heroes in providing the financial resources we need."

Get Information from Employees on the Front Lines

One challenge for high-level leaders in organizations is getting information about wrongdoing or exemplary behavior from employees. Camden has developed a novel approach to find out what goes on in the front line with his employees by making use of social media sites such as Facebook and LinkedIn. Although some companies' legal departments advise against this approach, Camden believes it is critical to get unbiased information. "I have a very good window as to how our behavior is being seen at the lowest ranks of the company," he says. "Having a sounding board from the lowest rank [employees], who are least willing to make excuses for bad corporate behavior I find to be useful. They often give me things to think about like how can you do 'x' while believing 'y.' Well, I never thought about it, so let's check it out."

Engage in Small Acts Speaking Volumes

Many leaders believe they need to engage in big actions to create the right culture and influence employees. At Kelly Services, small acts of good speak volumes. As Camden states, "Little symbolic actions that become part of the narrative of a corporation are very important to pay attention to." As an example, Camden saw on Facebook that an employee was upset. As a response, he called this employee, and after he convinced her of his true identity, he comforted her by discussing what was wrong and helping her feel valued. Such individualized behavior from organizational leaders is not always possible, but this story has been shared throughout the organization. Camden realizes, "Every person I do respond to directly is probably worth a hundred people hearing the story." The symbolic value of compassion cannot be overstated.

Be about Something Bigger

In the competitive business environment, bottom-line outcomes are of utmost importance. Although high performance matters, what really inspires employees is doing something that matters to the world. According to Camden, "It is really important that a company believes in something more than just simply making money. Kelly visibly joins a fight as to what is good for the society that we are embedded in or what is good for our workers, and we are aggressive for this fight." Led by their CEO, Carl Camden, Kelly Services is a wonderful example of a Fortune 500 company trying to do good in the world.

TWEETS

Ethics codes must be more than window dressing: ethical leaders live the code through their actions and by implementing ethical practices.

Doing good leads to doing well: employees of ethical leaders are more loyal, more satisfied, work harder, and perform better.

Ethical leaders not only punish the bad but embrace the good: rewarding ethical excellence creates loyal employees.

9

Imbue the Organization with a Higher Purpose

Robert E. Quinn and
Anjan V. Thakor

Many organizations perform below their potential. They are composed of self-interested people playing zero-sum games, pursuing external rewards, engaging in conflicts, and living in alienated relationships. Yet it is possible for those same people to willingly pursue the common good, to value intrinsic rewards, and to live in trust and experience high collaboration. This transformation occurs when a leader helps to imbue the organization with a higher purpose. Yet few executives understand how to do so. In this chapter we explain the barriers that block them from imbuing their organizations with a higher purpose, and we offer three strategies to help you do so.

A Higher Purpose

So what is a higher purpose, and why is it important? According to modern microeconomics, managers running organizations seek to solve the "principal-agent problem."[1] This problem occurs when a manager (principal) seeks to motivate an employee (agent) to work hard in the best interests of the manager.

This perspective assumes that if managers cannot continuously monitor their employees' activities, employees will behave in a purely self-interested manner. The manager will need to compensate the employee in a way to elicit the desired effort. The performance measurement and compensation packages, widely used in organizations, are based on this premise. Although these systems provide positive employee incentives to work hard, they are limited in their effectiveness and often fail to produce flourishing organizations.

In our own exploration of positive leadership, we began to question the logic of the principal-agent problem. Is there no alternative, other than to assume agents will only act in pure self-interest? We created a mathematical framework, extending the principal-agent model, introducing the notion of a higher purpose in a way that positively affects the behavior of both the manager and employee.[2]

Our definition of higher purpose is intent, perceived as producing a social benefit over and above the monetary payoff shared by the employer (principal) and employee (agent). It may be increased quality of life for some customer population, the preservation of some aspect of the environment, or some other commonly desired, collective good.

When the members of an organization sincerely pursue such a purpose, it produces increased meaning. Having a higher purpose makes the pursuit of profit more rewarding than just obtaining profit. The work begins to matter more to everyone.

An Economic Logic for Positive Leadership

Our analysis suggests managers that pursue higher purpose invest more capital, take greater risks, and incur lower costs of compensating their employees. When a leader commits to a higher purpose and inspires others to follow, the principal-agent problem is altered. Employees, embracing the higher purpose, are transformed: they derive positive value from their effort and act more like principals.

These effects imply that shirking can be overcome by the alignment of the employee with a higher purpose, providing incentives for the employee to work harder for the same compensation. However, authenticity is essential. A manager simply paying lip service to a higher purpose in order to "motivate" agents to work harder is unlikely to succeed. The lack of authenticity is likely to become apparent in subtle ways.

The economics of higher purpose do not negate the normal assumptions of economics. The model shows the pursuit of a higher purpose can be *joined* with the pursuit of wealth maximization, and they can each enhance the other. The main point is that the pursuit of a higher purpose generates positive energy in leaders and employees—a sort of off-balance-sheet asset. It substitutes for direct monetary incentives, increasing overall wealth, even when profit/wealth is not the object of pursuit. The reason is that the pursuit of a higher purpose generates additional satisfaction for those engaged in the effort, which makes it more enjoyable for all.

Why Pursue a Higher Purpose?

Our model is valuable, producing an economic logic for the pursuit of a higher purpose. Although our analysis does not provide large-sample empirical evidence, we have gathered anecdotal evidence from dozens of personal interviews with senior leaders supporting the theoretical model's findings. Moreover, much empirical evidence complements the model, making the case for the power of a higher purpose more convincing. But if you do not believe in the power of a higher purpose, you will not act with authenticity, and you will fail. We consider two core reasons that pursuit of a higher purpose is important: purpose and meaning, and purpose and emergent change.

Reason One: Purpose and Meaning

Purpose has value at the individual level. The literature suggests that a higher purpose leads to increased meaning and many benefits follow.

People who dedicate themselves to the realization of a higher purpose report higher levels of meaning in life and have higher scores on happiness, well-being, life satisfaction, life control, and work engagement; and lower scores on negative affect, depression, anxiety, being a workaholic, suicidal ideation, substance abuse, and the need for therapy.[3]

If the pursuit of a higher purpose produces benefits, why do not all leaders pursue it? The reason is that not all people are oriented to the articulation of collective purpose and creation of shared meaning. Only some people are "transformational leaders" likely to create organizations of higher purpose.[4]

Instead of relying on technical expertise, authority, and transactional power, transformational leaders operate from moral power. They move agents to a more intrinsic orientation, increased awareness of a higher purpose, and willingness to sacrifice for the common good.[5] Transformational leaders increase collective performance by creating congruence between the agent's and the organization's values.[6] In transforming people and organizations, leaders engage in four kinds of behavior:[7]

1. **Inspirational Motivation.** They articulate a higher purpose or vision, communicating the expectations that people can accomplish the purpose. They focus attention and motivate people to become engaged in purposeful action.
2. **Intellectual Stimulation.** They challenge existing assumptions, opening their followers' minds to new possibilities, purposes, and paths.
3. **Individualized Consideration.** They coach and mentor followers as valued people, giving attention, support, and encouragement. They build trust and belief.
4. **Idealized Influence.** They live with personal purpose, regulating by modeling integrity or inspiring values and beliefs. They attract the loyalty and commitment of followers.

Reason Two: Purpose and Emergent Change

Leaders who engage in these four behaviors are people of integrity. They articulate vision, stimulate learning, and build trust. Relational dynamics become more positive and animated, and new forms of organizing emerge.

Leaders who pursue a higher purpose achieve results following similar paths. Agents become empowered as they gain an increased sense of autonomy, competence, impact, and meaning.[8] As leaders elevate and develop more authentic and empowered agents, the inspirational process becomes reciprocal. The development of followers begins to reinforce the leader's development. The relationships of increased authenticity are more dynamic. They become self-reinforcing upward spirals.[9]

In the pursuit of a higher purpose, people may engage in the subordination of self-interest and willingly make spontaneous contributions to the whole. They are more likely to step away from their normal assumptions of hierarchy and limited contribution. They may begin to transcend job descriptions, share tacit information, create novel interpretations, and actively listen to one another.[10]

In the dynamics of transformative cooperation, the ratio of positive to negative thoughts and feelings may increase. The natural, downward spirals that normally turn organizations rigid may become upward spirals that promote learning, resilience, and the creation of new resources. The process may give rise to new and renewed relationships, further facilitating positive change.

Organizations of higher purpose benefit from many of these synergies and ones between stakeholders. An analysis of thirty Fortune 500 companies, identified as organizations having a higher purpose, demonstrated that these companies outperformed the market average by a ratio of 8 to 1.[11]

A Surprising Discovery

After building our higher-purpose model, we wondered how the heads of organizations work the process. We conducted thirty interviews, but with an incorrect assumption that all organization leaders would value having a higher purpose. The majority told us this assumption was not true. When they first took over, many did not see the value of having a higher purpose, some even belittling the notion.

This kind of behavior is predicted in the work of Peter Vaill, who points out that higher purpose must be "discovered, articulated, acted upon, and continually clarified." It is an ongoing process, requiring continual attention. Vaill writes, "In my own experience with management groups, I frequently encounter impatience, even exasperation, with discussions of basic purposes." He explains that managers wish to absolve themselves of the "responsibility to creatively revivify purposes."[12]

Our experience is consistent with Vaill's claim. Executives tend to be steeped in the assumptions of microeconomics: they are busy and hunger for task completion. The belief in the normal assumptions of microeconomics may lead to a focus on motivation, through the manipulation of external rewards. Creating meaning may seem like a waste of time. Pressure may lead to the search for easy tasks with high payoffs, not the grueling task of understanding the deep needs of stakeholders and articulating a vision. The need for task completion may work against the notion of continually monitoring and reformulating the meaning system. There is a natural pull for executives, even CEOs, to be managers rather than leaders.

This blindness is your opportunity. By understanding the logic of having a higher purpose and learning to pursue it, you can do things others cannot do.

Strategies for Imbuing Organizations with a Higher Purpose

Learning how to execute these strategies for becoming a positive leader who can imbue an organization with higher purpose will give you unique value. There are three key strategies to achieve this:

Strategy 1: Become a Person of Higher Purpose

It is common to find strategies in the management literature that leaders are supposed to impose on others. Because authenticity is critical to leadership, the first step in learning to create organizations of higher purpose is to become a person of higher purpose, which involves choosing your own higher purpose. A strategy for doing this revolves around a concept known as fundamental state of leadership (FSL),[13] which suggests leadership is not a function of position. Leadership is influence, and everyone has the potential for influence. How much influence is wielded at any given time varies, so leadership is not a set of traits. Leadership is influence, peaking when entering a more dynamic and elevated state, tied to a higher purpose.

People normally tend to be comfort-centered, externally directed, self-focused, and internally closed. The questions in Table 1 can be used to change those tendencies. By reaching this elevated state, one begins to find and pursue higher purposes (see the elevated consciousness associated with question three in Table 1).

One can learn and repeat the concepts in Table 1 in a matter of minutes, but this does not mean they can be applied. We have discovered people need assistance in internalizing them.

TABLE 1 The fundamental state of leadership as a path to higher purpose

Natural Default Options	FSL Questions	Elevated Consciousness	Consequences	Positive Self-Variations
Comfort-Centered	What result do I want to create?	Clarifies a desired future	Opens a new path of action	Acts of increased conviction
Externally Directed	Am I internally directed?	Clarifies personal values	Structures ethical boundaries	Acts of increased authenticity
Self-Focused	Am I other-focused?	Clarifies a purpose higher than self	Ignites trust	Acts of increased collaboration
Internally Closed	Am I externally open?	Clarifies need for feedback	Insures learning	Acts of increased cocreation

We invite people to anticipate coming events, ask the four questions, and envision possible positive self-variations. We have them act on their anticipated strategies, documenting the experiences that occur. The written accounts are called fundamental state of leadership best practices (FSLBPs).

Finally, we set up communities of learning. Participants agree to write one FSLBP each week. Each day, the community receives one or more of the written practices—which can be practical and inspiring. At the end of the week, each person submits a new FSLBP, and the process repeats. Over time, individuals learn to embrace higher purpose through a series of individual acts, and the sharing teaches the community to be more open to collectively pursuing higher purpose.

Strategy 2: Learn Vision Formulation

A key step in imbuing an organization with purpose is the creation of a meaningful vision, capturing and conveying higher intent.[14] These visions capture what is most important about the organization: how it relates to customers, employees, and others.[15] Visions are more influential if they are simple, idealistic, visual, long-term, challenging, and realistic. They should provide a sense of direction, related to the higher purpose of the organization. But they should be ambiguous enough to insure freedom and initiative.[16]

Developing such a vision is not a mechanical process, but requires a deep understanding of the organization, its culture, and people. The vision is likely to be more influential if the developers do the following:[17]

- Listen deeply to a wide array of stakeholders.
- Identify the most salient values and desires of stakeholders.
- Identify high-level strategic objectives with wide appeal.

- Understand, honor, and articulate the essence of the higher purpose.
- Show a link of the higher purpose to past achievements and current capacities.
- Continually monitor and refine the vision.

Strategy 3: Learn Vision Implementation

Formulating a meaningful vision is a difficult task, but it is only one step in the creation of organizations having a higher purpose. In implementing the vision,[18] leaders are more likely to succeed if they do the following:

- Hire and empower innovative people to pursue the higher purpose of the organization.
- Emphasize positivity and appreciation for flexibility and change.
- Encourage and reward learning.
- Update and develop the organization's mental models.
- Test proposed innovations with small-scale experiments.
- Monitor, examine, and learn from unexpected successes and failures.
- Emphasize and facilitate information sharing.
- Value and preserve past learning.
- Set objectives for innovative activities.
- Reward initiative and innovation.

Putting It All Together

Because normal economic assumptions often ignore higher purpose, we encourage positive leaders to develop a new logic. Most executives flee from their responsibility to lead their organizations with a higher purpose. Our strategies provide you with a way to be a positive leader, imbuing your organization with a higher purpose. Not only will you achieve the satisfaction of leading with character and values, but your company will likely also enjoy greater employee commitment and perform better financially.

THE BIRTH OF A HIGHER PURPOSE

A CEO at a large investment firm remembered being a young member of the company's executive team. They had a meeting with Peter Drucker, the famous theorist and consultant.

Drucker pushed the group to clarify the organization's purpose. The initial reaction was, "to make profits." Drucker would not accept this, pushing them to dig deeper. There was a politically correct conversation following his pushing, with the team growing impatient to move on. Drucker persisted. The former CEO finally grew angry, asking, "What else was the purpose of the corporation, other than to pursue profits?" Drucker was not intimidated, continuing to push.

Eventually, they articulated the company's purpose: something quite different from the pursuit of profit. They defined the purpose as helping to serve the needs of their clients and taking care of their families and loved ones. Clients are interested in tax planning and investment advice, to preserve and grow their wealth so they can care for and educate their families. Clients do not pursue wealth just for the sake of it—they want to help their families lead more fulfilling lives.

This new perspective on their purpose meant the organization had to reorient itself. It first had to understand client needs and then tailor financial advice to serve those needs—instead of trying to sell financial products to maximize profits. The use of the word "profit" is no longer part of the organization's lexicon.

The company's positive culture and unusual success today is attributed to defining the organization's higher purpose. Clarifying the purpose transformed the principal-agent problem. The employees of the company do not have to receive special financial incentives to have this client orientation. It has become part of the culture, the natural thing to do.

TWEETS

Creating an organizational purpose that is higher than profit makes the pursuit of profit more rewarding and transforms the meaning of work.

In organizations of higher purpose, people transcend job descriptions, share information, have unique insights, and carefully listen to one another.

Imbuing an organization with a higher purpose requires discovering, articulating, acting upon, and continually clarifying the purpose.

IV

CREATE RESOURCEFUL CHANGE

Your leadership requires constant engagement with change. This section offers important insights about how to engage these change processes in ways that create rather than diminish resources. It is an exciting prospect to consider how the challenge of change initiation and implementation can be transformed into an opportunity for new resource creation. This section breaks open new ways of seeing and implementing change that alerts the trajectory of possibilities for enhancing your and the organization's capacity for excellence. Our contributors invite you to examine how you look for and engage with hope, how you see and foster discovery, how you treat employees as resources, and how you engage crises with a mindset of opportunities. Be prepared to enhance the zone of possibility for enlarging the difference you can make as a leader by viewing and engaging change in these ways.

10

Cultivate Hope:
Found, Not Lost

Oana Branzei

Hope is a common, mundane experience, a deep belief that people and situations can and will change—for the better. Everyone hopes, some of the time. However, the consistent and persistent cultivation of hope is a virtuous and noteworthy undertaking.[1] At full strength hope can be heroic, even transformational. As President Obama explained, hope is "imagining and then fighting for and struggling for and sometimes dying for what didn't seem possible before."[2]

As a way of seeing, feeling, and being, hope has fundamentally changed the course of human history. Hope has been practiced over space and time, called forth by political leaders such as Mahatma Gandhi and Nelson Mandela, preached by religious leaders like Mother Theresa and Archbishop Desmond Tutu, and harnessed into thriving organizations by modern-day business leaders like Virgin founder Richard Branson or Grameen Bank founder Muhammad Yunus.[3] Once they believed that a better future was forthcoming, these leaders actively searched for human potentiality and acted repeatedly and persistently to promote human betterment, even in the midst of adversity.

The cultivation of hope by exemplary leaders models how any leader can lead with hope, rather than without it. This chapter is about cultivating hope at work: a guide to how you too can find lost hope in your organization, how to hold on to hope in the midst of despair, not letting it fade or decay over time, and spreading it as broadly as possible. On the jagged roller coaster of life's unavoidable ups and downs, leaders who cultivate hope never lose heart or sight of the future they are after. To lead with hope is to know when you are about to lose it—and work to earn it right back. To sense the fullness of hope approaching—yet be on the lookout for the next bump along the road. Leveraging the author's three decades of research in philosophy, sociology, anthropology, psychology, and business, this chapter introduces hope as a "powerful leadership tool" and a "sustainable form of human motivation."[4]

The Value of Hope

In its broadest definition, hope is "a way of feeling, a way of thinking, a way of behaving, and a way of relating to oneself and to one's world." This definition emphasizes the four different ways in which hope recharges us. Affectively, hope is an energizing force that "propels persons forward when the odds seem against them." Cognitively, hope fortifies people who have found a way and helps them improvise work-arounds when the way no longer works. Behaviorally, hope involves an active search for possible and appropriate ways to get to one's goal. Spiritually, hope helps us "rise above difficult circumstances" and "find one's soul."[5]

Across cultures, measures, and methods, hope is the will to keep searching for something better, especially when clear ways to get there from here are still unclear, unavailable, or unfeasible. Hope enables leaders to press on and boldly go where they really want to, not merely where they know they can. Hope opens us to imagine unexpected possibilities. It energizes our striving for more, even in extremely stressful and strenuous circumstances.[6] And it often endures, until the hoped-for outcome is achieved.

Hope's main function is to ignite and sustain action toward future goals, to move individuals and collectives onward into a risky and often underresourced future. Hope allows us to hang on to cherished goals and ideals long enough to figure out how we may attain them. Thus it is an "emergency virtue" helping us to deal with challenging situations.[7]

Cultivating hope helps leaders imprint and sustain forward momentum for their organizations, when the future they want is really hard to attain. Hope helps leaders become "unreasonable," namely, to pursue goals they deem worthwhile by being unencumbered by current means.[8] Hope is found at the root of radical prosocial organizing and is conspicuous in the genesis of radical business models that alleviate human suffering and repair or reverse environmental damage.

Over the last thirty years, we have accumulated many helpful insights about the presence and the influence of hope for individuals, organizations, communities, and societies[9] by studying the psychological underpinnings of hope, philosophies of hope, vocabularies of hope, even pedagogies for inviting and sustaining hope. Some of us already enjoy the many positive consequences of hope, from meeting the most basic needs for survival and dignity, to improvements in our education, health, and engagement at work—where hope betters our self-confidence, clarity, creativity, work ethic, and productivity.[10] But we can definitely do more to cultivate hope at work, especially in difficult times. The three principles I introduce and illustrate help leaders resuscitate, redirect, and renew hope. The sidebar at the end of this chapter showcases two leaders who combine all three principles to habitually find lost hope—and help many others do the same.

Three Principles and Practices of Cultivating Hope

These three principles speak to, and tap into, our innate capacity, even necessity, to hope for something better for everyone and in every circumstance. First, we need to imagine the future we want and hold onto it just long enough so we can take the very first small step in its direction. Second, we need to look out, and compensate in whatever little ways we can, for any obstacles along the way that may delay or divert the pursuit of hope. Third, we need continuous reminders of the hope that already exists elsewhere so we can help our hope persist a while longer. Leaders like you can bring each principle to life by engaging, and role modeling, in one simple practice: acting "as if" the imagined future is within reach; helping out employees who fall down or lose their way along the journey; and continuously piecing together any acts of hope you find scattered and spread throughout the organization to create and sustain the perception of a continuous stream of hope at work.

Hope Principle 1: Act "As If"

Cultivating hope is all about taking action, right now—but not just any action. Former IDEO associate partner, innovation consultant, and entrepreneur Thomas Stat practices, and recommends to everyone, acting exactly as "if the future were guaranteed."[11] Taking even the smallest of steps keeps one's hope alive. It also ranks worthwhile but hard-to-achieve goals as priorities and constantly (re)aligns one's experiences and relationships with the structure of one's faith, beliefs, and values in life. Taking action "as if" the desired goal was possible helps overcome the inertia of the status quo and conquers the initial fear of the unknown, complex, and difficult road ahead. Acts are powerful wellsprings of hope. They rekindle one's motivation to move forward and enact their will although no ways are available—yet.

Acting "as if" keeps our sense of possibility alive. Even the simplest and smallest of acts resurrect hope, by awakening and aligning our cognitive, affective, behavioral, and spiritual capabilities with a cherished but often distant goal. Muhammad Yunus asked, "What if you could harness the power of the free market to solve the problems of poverty, hunger, and inequality?"[12] And then he began acting "as if" he really could. Hopeful leaders do not merely ask "What If?" but also begin acting "as if" the future they want were sure to shortly come their way.

No act is too small to resuscitate hope. Any steps that keep us searching in the right direction prepare and enable us to discern the future we want—or at least get us unstuck from an unwanted place. Some steps, such as resistance or protest acts, may help us hang on to the little hope we still have. Others, such as making promises, questioning naysayers, or gathering allies, keep us running in place until the right opportunities, capabilities, and technologies finally open up.

Great change often has humble beginnings.[13] Nelson Mandela's small acts of protest are famous for igniting world-changing hope. In prison Mandela was issued short pants because he was a black South African[14] while prisoners of other ethnicities received long pants—along with better meals and treatment. Mandela repeatedly asked for long pants, and "after complaining for a week, he woke up to find a pair of pants in his cell. [But] he noticed that no one else had them in his prison, so he gave them back."[15] Then he kept on protesting. "We put our foot down and insisted on being respected," he explained. Mandela acted "as if" throughout his twenty-seven years in prison and continued to do so afterward. Acting "as if" gave Mandela the "courage to do better than your best."[16]

But hope is not always humble. Ray Anderson was the founder and chairman of Interface, Inc., a $1.1 billion carpet company, until his death in 2011. Anderson's 1994 "promise to eliminate any negative impact our company may have on the environment by the year 2020" (mission-zero)[17] was boastful and deemed mission impossible for the next decade. But Anderson persisted, and by 2009, he was already halfway there. By 2011, Anderson not only reversed his company's "pillaging and damaging the land," but also created one of the first pro-environmental business consultancies that helped industry peers and other leaders make and keep similar promises. His thousand-plus speeches influenced generations of leaders to follow suit. Many who initially doubted his promise have since set their own mission-zero targets, and some have already achieved them.

Any leader can act "as if," using small protests and/or large promises, to resuscitate hope at work.

Hope Principle 2: "Kiss It Better"

Bearing witness to human pain and suffering wears hope thin. Even organizations specializing in sustaining hope may lose it at times.[18] Hopeful leaders are no strangers to hopelessness, but any dips are short lived because they act swiftly to catch and reverse downfalls. They believe in miracles, just enough to make some happen. They remember, retell, and relive successful reversals, dwelling on the happiest of endings to the most challenging of situations. They replay and rehearse what went well, often collectively and publicly, and down-play the myriad other factors that could well have gotten in the way.

Hopelessness invites and welcomes relief. Leaders can re-store and shore up hopefulness by contrasting moments of de-spair with less visible but longer-lasting skills, strengths, and especially dreams of better times ahead. They can also fend off the erosion of hope and temper sudden drops by offering persuasive, frequent, even routinized, reminders to (re)focus on the positive and to keep moving forward even when a step back might have been unavoidable.

Globally practiced by mothers and fathers, this "kiss it better" approach has been shown to swiftly and effectively re-direct hopelessness to hopefulness in hospitals, schools, even in the aftermath of disasters.[19] The approach is simple, but not trivial. Because redirections are more effective when remedies are delivered immediately and persuasively, leaders often need to foresee and prepare for different contingencies so they can be prepared; they must be able, willing, and ready to reach out for hopeful stories, scripts, and supports anytime or any-place a redirection may be called for.

In postgenocide Rwanda, widows used to "struggle most of the time, . . . when we have children, . . . teach them that hap-piness doesn't exist, that there is no pure love and, as legacy, we give them our despair, our debts, our doubts, our tears, our failures."[20] In 2005, Odile Gakire Katese, fondly known as Kiki, founded Ingoma Nshya, Rwanda's first and only group of women drummers. Sharing stories, moving together, and mak-ing loud, energizing music week after week created a pre-dictable and highly effective reversal. Now over one hundred strong, the world-acclaimed troupe is so hopeful that it reignites others' hope. Then Katese founded Inzozi Nziza, the country's first and only ice cream parlor, creating a sharp contrast that deliberately invited hope back in, not just for the widows, but also for everyone struggling with bouts of hopelessness. She said, "We want to share moments that are not embossed by despair and death. . . . We want to create a space where poverty, disease, illiteracy . . . are not obstacles to happiness and barriers between human beings."

In New York City, Lisa Honig Buksbaum, CEO and founder of Soaring Words,[21] works to shore up bouts of hopelessness for hospitalized children fighting for their life and their worry-stricken parents. Buksbaum has helped 250,000 families thus far. She invites tenfold more healthy children and grown-ups to contribute multiple visual, verbal, and textured messages of hope, from cards and poems to vividly decorated warm quilts. These remind sick children of their strength and dreams, so they do not run out of hope when they need it the most.

Although music, ice cream, and quilts may often work, leaders can choose from a variety of organizational tools and artifacts to "kiss it better" when something bad happens at work. There are moments when clients are lost, opportunities missed, cherished projects fall through, or relationships unravel. Leaders need to recognize the lapse in hope, and before hopelessness sets in, swiftly call on—preferably publicly and vividly—reminders of everyone's already proven ability to see the current challenge through.

Hope Principle 3: "Shared, Not Stored"

Hope is renewable. The more it flows, the more it becomes cognitively, affectively, behaviorally, and spiritually energizing. But hope does not renew automatically or effortlessly. Leaders need to know the people, projects, and places where hope naturally occurs and pools—there, the future looks a little closer and brighter; forthcoming events are infused with possibilities, and projects are steeped in expectations of success rather than failure; "can't do" is unheard of because everyone is ready, even anxious, to take a step ahead and is looking forward to what is coming next. Then leaders deliberately tap these hope pools by staging opportunities for contagion. Activities such as spontaneous get-togethers and impromptu contests help hope flow. Hopeful exchanges can set off chain reactions: sharing unexpected opportunities or revealing positive surprises spark additional "as if" acts that put new hope cycles in motion.

Remember that hope is asking for nothing but the will to see or to do things differently; the forward momentum enabled by such will can release constraints, reveal new paths or even build them against the odds. It is not how much further one looks, but how much more hopeful one is about eventually getting there, that betters one's odds of finding the way there. However hopeful you are as a leader, yours is but one will; share it with hundreds, thousands, even millions and watch your odds turn in your favor.

Ela R. Bhatt founded the Self-Employed Women's Association (SEWA) in 1972 to serve the 94 percent of the working women in India who lacked any prospects of fair, let alone formal, employment. More than a million women, whom Bhatt calls her "sisters," pooled their hope together. First they imagined what could be possible in the future. Then they acted on each possibility, developing the skills they needed to match their unmet needs. As their numbers grew, so did their needs and their skills. SEWA is now a network of self-sustaining enterprises and a fast-growing movement.[22] Like Bhatt, hopeful leaders do not let hope sit idle. As soon as they muster some hope, they stir it up to multiply manifold the few possibilities they foresee.

Putting It All Together

Cultivating hope at work matters because doing so focuses leadership attention on the possibilities ahead. It helps everyone else see beyond the many obstacles, even setbacks, unavoidably awaiting them along the way, so they can get going toward making their dreams come true. There is undeniable magic in bringing someone's hope up, but in this chapter we revealed three simple strategies well within every leader's reach. With practice, the magic of hope can become a way of life even in organizations that face significant pain or struggle. So we invite you to raise some hope at work, starting today. If times are particularly tough, start by acting "as if" hope is just around the corner. This will help you hold fast and keep looking for ways forward, even as your organization is being buffeted by waves of hopelessness. If you are already catching glimpses of hope, welcome them and work hard through repeated reminders and personal touches so the flame of possibility does not get prematurely extinguished. And once you have gotten the flame of hope burning bright, give it plenty of fuel so it spreads throughout your organization.

CULTIVATING HOPE AT FREE THE CHILDREN AND ME TO WE

Free the Children and Me to We are sister ventures, the nonprofit and for-profit arms of a single entity cofounded by two brothers, Craig and Marc Kielburger. Both ventures were "as if" acts. After reading about the gruesome execution of a boy his own age, Craig Kielburger, then age twelve, stood up in class and asked his classmates to join him and fight together against child slavery. Eleven said yes, and Free the Children was instantly born. A decade ago, Me to We was deliberately designed to enable "thousands of people who believe in social change" to also act "as if" because they wanted to transform customers "into world-changers, one action and experience at a time."[23]

Craig and Marc Kielburger redirect hope at both ends of the spectrum: striving to improve childhoods around the world by improving the lives of those living in poverty with the resources they badly need and enriching the lives of those living in abundance with causes they can care deeply about. Every transaction is a crafted contrast, simultaneously restoring hope for the givers and receivers. And they renew hope not only by tapping into pools of hope, but by creating proprietary cascades where it flows abundantly and freely among prestigious or popular speakers and large audiences. Through the movement "We Day,"[24] their organization is now millions strong across traditional media, TV networks, and online forums, and Craig and Marc Kielburger host a series of large-scale annual gatherings where young social agents swap stories and share experiences. Their hope continues to flourish long after the events, (re)kindled by songs, dances, and memories that go viral across different media. Carefully crafted and supported linkages before, during, and after these events help (re)circulate hope among existing pools and encourage the emergence of new pools, inside and outside the organization.

TWEETS

Now is a good time to fight off hopelessness.

Hopeful leaders believe in miracles, just enough to make some happen.

Dwell on the happiest of endings to the most challenging of situations.

11

Create Micro-moves for Organizational Change

Karen Golden-Biddle

Recall an organizational change you have personally experienced and considered important to implement. How did you come to see this change as desired and viable? How did people undertake meaningful and collaborative effort? How was energy generated to keep going? Questions such as these direct our attention toward the "how" of change: actions and interactions comprising change processes that, while small and often barely visible, are essential to the successful creation of generative change. We call them "micro-moves."[1]

Usually, we pay attention to the "what" of organizational change (e.g., structural reorganization, incentive schemes, leadership turnover) and leave implicit the micro-moves comprising the "how" of change. The press showcases dramatic examples of "what" changes. At the time of this writing, the change to Microsoft's organization structure is front page news—a change made to encourage collaboration and "move from multiple Microsofts to one Microsoft," in the words of CEO Steve Ballmer.[2] Yet beyond the announcement and commentary on the merits or potential difficulties of this particular structural shift, we learn little about how this large-scale, top-down directed change will be implemented to accomplish the vision of one

Microsoft with greater collaboration. Structural change itself does not ensure generative change of the type envisioned in their goal of "collaboration."

Research suggests that our process of changing organizations is equally important to what is changed, and that how we change organizations significantly shapes the pathway for desired change and the extent to which collective energy, direction, and enthusiasm can be cultivated to create and to sustain such change.[3] The present chapter builds on this research to make the case for why organizations and individuals, especially leaders of change at all levels, should care about micro-moves. Then, focusing on the earliest origins of change—when hunches and feelings suggest the need to change, but no real sense exists regarding what might inform the shape of change—the chapter closely examines a specific set of micro-moves of discovery that help seed generative change by engaging people in collective imagining of the desired possible.

Why Do Micro-moves Matter in Change?

Micro-moves, though small, are consequential for generating or derailing change efforts. We have all experienced micro-moves and their effects: those interactions that foster disengagement, inciting disbelief that desired change will ever really happen, and by contrast, those interactions that facilitate engagement, inciting a collective sense of hope that one's effort will make a difference in achieving change[4] and initiating a "cascading vitality" for change[5] through employee empowerment. Micro-moves of the latter kind matter to leadership practice because they engage people meaningfully and respectfully in the change process. In turn, a higher level of psychological engagement with the change is fostered along with enhanced capability to stretch beyond one's comfort zone in realizing the desired change.

Micro-moves also matter because they help embolden individuals to see new ways to connect with others in creating change. We see this in the impact of being what some researchers call tempered radicals,[6] insiders who identify with and are committed to their organization while also committed to an issue that can be at odds with their organization. For example, rather than push their agendas and issues, these insiders enact more tempered micro-moves such as subtle self-expression of issues or strategic alliances with like-minded others. Similarly, we see the impact of being issue sellers,[7] individuals committed to an issue who try to convince others to pay attention to or resource the issues. One study of issue sellers shows how these individuals seek to engage others through generative rather than antagonistic dialogue, drawing attention to productive differences that widen and enrich rather than shut down conversation, keeping alive the possibility of change.[8]

Micro-moves of Discovery

The earliest origins of generative organizational change call upon people to imagine what could be—what might be possible. Micro-moves of discovery nourish this collective imagining by engaging us to notice and to reconsider our taken-for-granted assumptions and expectations of how things are currently done and of what currently seems viable and comfortable.[9] They not only produce a wider range of ideas and possibilities, they also foster momentum for launching change and enhance human capability for dealing with uncertainty. In this section, I offer three micro-moves of discovery for use in change efforts to enable the collective imagining of desired possibilities. All three operate by asking people to connect or to experience what they find familiar in light of something unfamiliar, thus creating an atypical or even surprising relation that can illuminate prevailing expectations.

Micro-move 1: Turn Toward the Unfamiliar

Although this particular micro-move of discovery may be implemented in a variety of ways, its distinguishing feature is the request of people to turn toward and explore rather than dismiss what is unfamiliar in order to see and to reconsider expectations about current ways of operating.

We implement this micro-move in everyday conversation when we ask questions in the subjunctive, rather than indicative, mood. Whereas the indicative draws attention to what we do know (e.g. "what is . . ."), the subjunctive illuminates contingency and possibility based in what we do not yet know (e.g., "what if . . ." or "what might be . . ."). For example, instead of asking, "What is a phone used for?," Apple designers of the iPhone might well have asked, "What if we could do more than talk on a phone?" We also have the opportunity to implement this micro-move when we seek customer, student, or client input on our services and products. We capitalize on this opportunity when we explore input that we find odd or surprising and use our exploration to discover what we do not know and to shed light on how this new insight might be used to change our services or products.

Organizations such as Google in the software industry implemented this micro-move by relating the then-familiar notion of "software as product" with the unfamiliar image of "software as service." Instead of seeing software as a product in a box purchased by consumers to install on their computers, imagining software as a service opened up the possibility of an alternative delivery model of hosting software on a cloud space that is available on demand to customers. In creating this atypical connection, they were able to reimagine the meaning of software and generate new uses and applications. Although today it sounds commonplace to think of software as a service, at the time some organizations dismissed the idea.

Micro-move 2: Experience Together What Is Not Known

The second micro-move of discovery is grounded in the recognition that discovery can require more than the cognitive work of questioning and gathering input central in the first micro-move. Often, we may not notice or may have only an unspecified sense or niggling feeling about what needs to change. Thus, this second micro-move asks people to collectively experience what they do not know.

A medium-sized health-care system used this micro-move early in creating a novel inpatient care system known as "Collaborative Care" that has subsequently received national attention.[10] Its use helped specify what staff knew only in a general sense: although how patients were admitted into hospital units was understood, the path leading to patient discharge was anything but clear. The hospital CEO gathered managers and administrative clinicians and posed the seemingly straightforward question: How do our patients leave our system? This group might have taken any number of steps to address the question, including conducting a literature search on best practices in inpatient care or charting current patient flow based on their collective knowledge. However, because this group had little contact with frontline care delivery, it is unlikely that these abstract actions would have helped them discover what they did not know about their own system.

Wanting to see close up the actual care path for their patients, the group decided instead to walk this path, first as if they were patients and then as observers alongside real patients. In taking this step, they began to experience together what they did not know. With the assistance of an organizational development consultant, the group adopted the stance of curious learner rather than expert to get the best possible access to the patient experience of care delivery. For example, clinicians ditched their medical frocks and managers took off their suit jackets. They also generated open-ended questions that focused on better understanding the care path from the patient's perspective. During their observations, a particularly revealing situation was disclosed that no one had noticed before: their patients were required to walk too long of a distance to undergo prescribed tests. With deep chagrin and embarrassment, they now could see that the walk was far too arduous for elderly people and very ill patients. In experiencing together the undue burdens placed on patients by their system, they came to collectively know what they all wanted to change and engaged in designing the new "Collaborative Care" model focused centrally on the patient's rather than the provider's experience.

Micro-move 3: Convene around New Possibilities

The third micro-move involves convening people for the purpose of exploring possibilities for change that have been discovered and are beginning to form as new ideas, early product designs, and as new ways of working. In convening, people listen for ways to give these emergent possibilities further shape.

Creating curriculum change in a university setting can be one of the most challenging and politically fraught changes leaders can attempt. A management school drew on this micro-move to help infuse ethics into its newly designed Master of Business Administration (MBA) curriculum. After launching a successful pilot course on ethics, the next step was to bring ethics into required courses. Yet, faculty teaching these courses (Finance, Marketing, etc.) expressed concern about being able to infuse ethics while also covering course material. A dean responsible for curriculum innovation convened a meeting of faculty teaching ethics as well as those teaching the required courses around the possibility of ethics infusion. During the ensuing conversation, many ideas emerged about how faculty might infuse ethics. One particular idea got traction because it recognized the concern that most faculty members are not ethics experts and at the same time crystallized faculty skill in holding class discussions. Faculty taking part in this conversation became energized as they began to conceive of facilitating discussion as a viable vehicle for ethics infusion in required courses and to generate specific questions for use in their classes.

Putting It All Together

Creating micro-moves in change matters because doing so focuses leadership attention on how, not just what, change is implemented and illuminates the significance of micro-moves that facilitate respectful and meaningful engagement of each other in the change process. Focusing on the early beginnings of generative change, we profiled the particular micro-moves of discovery that nourish collective imagining of new possibilities by helping us to become aware of and reconsider our implicit expectations about how things are currently done. We invite you to try some of these micro-moves for discovery to seed generative change in your personal lives and at work.

CREATING SUSTAINABLE MICRO-MOVES OF DISCOVERY: W. L. GORE AND ASSOCIATES, A COMPANY WHERE COLLECTIVE IMAGINING FLOURISHES

Founded in 1958 by Bill and Vieve Gore with the goal of "creating a company that would be a multiplier of human imagination,"[11] W. L. Gore and Associates (hereafter, "Gore") today is one of the two hundred largest privately held companies in the United States, achieving more than $3 billion in sales during the last fiscal year. It is best known for its innovative products using fluoropolymers (e.g., Gore-Tex) and for its organizational culture that couples teamwork and nonhierarchical structure with personal initiative. As Jack Cramer, Gore's Global Technology leader described, "Gore's business model is not a low-cost one. We look for the toughest problems to solve in an environment designed to drive creative, independent thinking in an atmosphere that fosters teamwork."[12]

A number of articles written about Gore portray the creation of generative change that contributes to the company's success. For example, the company continues to innovate in product lines and industries served (e.g., Gore-Tex garments, medical implants, coated guitar strings) and to support development of capabilities for cross-functional teamwork and imagination. The following examples from Gore illustrate how using the micro-moves of discovery profiled in this chapter help to seed generative change by engaging people in collective imagining of possibilities. Significantly, the examples demonstrate that micro-moves of discovery can be sustained by institutionalizing them in novel roles and everyday practices such as recruitment.

Micro-move 1 prompts people to turn toward and explore rather than dismiss the unfamiliar and what is not known. Expressed first in its founding principle of creating a company that "would be a multiplier of human imagination," Micro-move 1 is now alive in its hiring practices; Gore is quite up front about the fact that they want to hire people who are willing to explore the unfamiliar. This objective is signaled in company leader interviews such as the one with HR leader Donna Frey, who shared that the people Gore recruit "have got to be able to embrace uncertainty."[13] A visit to the company's website section on careers also signals the importance of being comfortable with considering and exploring the unfamiliar.[14] Asking potential applicants to consider if Gore is a good fit for them, the website identified questions that "outline [their] expectations of Gore Associates." For example, "Do you . . .

1. experiment with different approaches or solutions to improve the way things are done?"
2. challenge traditional thinking and identify creative approaches or solutions?"
3. maintain a high standard of performance in uncertain or unstructured situations?"
4. voice differences of opinion openly and directly?"

Micro-move 2 recognizes that we may only have an unspecified sense of what needs to change. As a result, experiencing together what is not known can help bring clarity to what is currently done and open the way to generating possibilities for change. A well-known way Gore implements this micro-move is through the practice of "dabbling," which not only allocates up to 10 percent of associates' time to developing new ideas but provides a sponsor who gives guidance and a cross-functional oversight group to check in periodically on the dabblings. Together, they experience the development of dabbling, being committed to protecting the origins, and assessing along the way the worthiness of each dabbling for further development and investment. This practice has led to many of Gore's breakthrough products and the company's entry into "new, untested markets [in which they have] seized the lead."[15]

Micro-move 3 involves convening people around new possibilities now represented by forms such as ideas, early product designs, and practices in order to contribute to their further development. One way Gore enacts this micro-move is by recognizing a type of leader whose responsibility it is to organize teams around new possibilities such as new businesses, products, and processes. Known as "Intrapreneuring Associates,"[16] they invite and convene associates to further consider these new possibilities. A second way this micro-move is implemented is through the monthly technical meeting,[17] which began in the early 1990s. Hundreds of associates come together from across teams and divisions to address those attending and also to learn from others about the latest ideas surfacing in their work.

TWEETS

Micro-moves of organizational change help leaders engage people meaningfully and respectfully in the change process.

Discovery micro-moves use collective experience to prompt questions about "what is" and to foster imagining of what might be possible.

By inviting people from across the organization to collaborate in discovery, micro-moves build collective energy and enthusiasm for change.

12

Treat Employees as Resources, Not Resisters

Scott Sonenshein

L ike most leaders, you have likely participated in and probably helped shape some type of organizational change, whether a
reorganization, new information technology system, or compliance with different regulations. Organizations routinely undergo change, but the disappointing reality is they routinely fail
to implement change effectively.[1] Leaders often blame employees for change unraveling, claiming employees resist change—
or even outright sabotage it.[2] Such a viewpoint is not grounded
in fact. It is also practically dangerous. By treating employees as
resisters to change, leaders can create a self-fulfilling prophecy
that *turns* them into resisters. Instead of thinking of employees
as change resisters, you need to think of them as valuable resources to help them initiate and implement change. By considering employees as resources, you enlist an often eager group
of individuals who recognize that the status quo is more dangerous than an unknown future. Although there is often inevi-
tably a handful of resisters in any organization, you need to be
careful not to let these distractions sidetrack you from focusing
on the more important task at hand: turning employees into
resources for change.

The Importance of Being Resourceful

Although organizations frequently need to change, leaders often have limited resources. During periods of decline, organizations may not have the critical resources needed to foster important strategic renewal. Or leaders may be reluctant to invest what precious resources they do have for change.[3] During good times, leaders may hesitate to foster organizational change, arguing the status quo is working just fine. Employees are often caught at the crossroads of this situation: asked to continuously adapt, but often not provided sufficient resources to do so. Worse off, leaders often blame employees for resisting change, overlooking their own culpability.[4] This blame game may create the very resistance leaders are attempting to eliminate. But by changing the story from "employees resist change" to "employees are resources for change," you can become more resourceful by unlocking the potential of employees instrumental to the success of change.

Being "resourceful" describes how leaders and employees take actions to make things more valuable—whether those things include material resources, such as products and factories, or immaterial resources, such as relationships. For example, viewing employees as resources and not resisters during change makes employees more valuable as they become enrolled in trying to change the organization versus working against it. The following section offers three strategies for employees to become more resourceful during organizational change initiatives; these are followed by three corresponding practices for leaders to transform employees from resisters to resources for change.

Three Strategies to Become More Resourceful During the Implementation of Change

This section describes three strategies for employees to become more resourceful when implementing change: "cut off the straps," storytelling the big picture and benefits, and integrate self-affirmation with doubt. These three strategies are complementary approaches.

Strategy 1: "Cut Off the Straps"

Being resourceful during change includes taking items that might appear to be of limited value and turning them into something to help implement change.[5] Individuals have a tendency to view a resource as a fixed entity.[6] For example, people might think a chair is something you sit on, but it can be used in countless ways: from stepstool to exercise equipment. Entrepreneurs, whose nascent organizations wrestle with change on a daily basis, often take critical resources other organizations do not value and make them into something useful.[7] My own research has found that rank-and-file employees are amazingly resourceful in transforming objects of seemingly inferior value into something extraordinary.[8] This capacity for resourcefulness allows employees to generate change, even when their options appear limited.

An example of Strategy 1 involves a retail store manager named Ethan who worked for a chain of women's clothing and accessory stores. He received a dress of suspect quality that was not selling very well at this store. Other stores in the chain also struggled in selling this dress, leading to a potentially large inventory write-off—just as the organization was hoping to grow. Ethan, as the leader of his store, decided to cut off the straps of the dress and relabel it, changing both its physical appearance and meaning. As a result, Ethan turned the dud of a dress into a best-selling beach cover-up. The founder of the company phoned Ethan to ask how his store accomplished what no other store could: he sold the inferior "dress." Ethan replied that he worked with the materials at hand, in the best possible way, recounting how he both physically altered the dress and then relabeled the dress as beachwear. Ethan also did not consider his role as fixed and instead transformed his role, at least temporarily, into a product designer. Ethan's story offers a lot of wisdom for change in other organizations. Often, employees think they lack the necessary resources to implement change, such as during a restructuring when they may be left with fewer employees to do more work in their groups. Instead of viewing everything as fixed, employees can identify their own "straps" and cut them off, thereby reinterpreting their roles and resources at hand in the face of seemingly formidable challenges.

Strategy 2: Storytelling the Big Picture and Benefits

When leaders consider employees as resources instead of as resisters, they no longer primarily view their role as motivating employees to change and, especially, not to resist change. Sure, motivation is often important for action, but the story shifts in a dramatic way. Employees can create their own motivation to implement change. In a study of entertainment product retail clerks, employees were found to be remarkably capable of creating the motivational resources that can foster effective change implementation: efficacy, a sense they can perform what is needed for the change; commitment, a desire to implement the change; and identification, attachment to their organization.[9] Employees create these resources by the stories they tell themselves and others about change. These stories have two main properties. First, they place the change in the context of the organization's larger strategy, which allows employees to understand the general direction in which the organization is heading. Second, they find the silver lining in the change by reinterpreting any potential disruption to their work routines, relationships, or practices in a way that can create benefits for the employee or organization.[10]

Let us consider two employees who worked at the same location of a large multinational chain of entertainment stores. The first person will be called "Rebecca Resister." When asked about the organization's strategic change, which involved integrating two operating divisions, Rebecca told the following story: "What is the point? Our store is just not big enough to [successfully implement the change]. . . . It's harmful to the company because it raises customer expectations to a level that we cannot support. . . . As for the future, I don't think much will change." No doubt Rebecca will be working hard to protect the status quo, not so much because she is a bad employee, but rather because she does not understand the benefits of the change and its larger purpose. Without focusing on the big picture and its benefits, Rebecca lacks efficacy, commitment, and identification—critical motivational resources to spark action to implement change. Now consider "Betty Believer." Betty works at the same store as Rebecca, but tells a radically different story of the change: "I enjoy the fresh appearance of the new store. I also like the increased impact the . . . marketing has on our store [such as] customer recognition of the . . . brand. . . . It also helps align . . . stores to the marketing and promotions used by the [rest] of the company." Betty rates substantially higher on the three motivational resources because she has integrated into her story of change the benefits of the change and its larger purpose.

Strategy 3: Integrate Self-Affirmation with Doubt

During change, employees often ask themselves questions that focus on uncertainty and doubt: Will my organization improve? How will my job change? What will happen to our culture? These are important and natural questions to ask. But employees who are resourceful ask an even more important question: What contribution can I make to help implement the change? Even employees who approach change from this proactive stance often struggle with a sense that their contribution will never be enough, no matter what they do to advance change. Unquestionably, change involves significant work on the part of employees who sometimes feel despair despite the best of intentions. But some employees can overcome this despair.

In the extreme example of environmental change agents, research has found that these change agents often take incredible action to advance environmental issues, from walking to work, to constantly pushing their colleagues to recycle, to trying to convince top managers to make their organizations greener. Nevertheless, these change agents often doubt whether they are doing enough. But alongside this doubt came a remarkable finding: these same change agents also frequently affirm themselves in such statements as "I have the experience, knowledge, and values to be a good environmentalist."[11]

This counterintuitive mix of self-assurance and self-criticism can help employees become more motivated to implement change. On their own, high doubts are bad because they freeze employees' action, stifling them with the enormity of the task at hand. But resourceful employees use low forms of doubt to create resources around urgency, springing themselves and others into action to institute change. These doubts serve as gentle reminders of improvements employees can make by having them question whether they are doing enough to advance change. During change, convincing organizations' members of the urgency for change is the most important aspect of starting a change initiative.[12] At the same time, resourceful employees constantly affirm themselves, serving as an antidote to their doubts and helping them see themselves as valuable change agents with something important to contribute.

Three Leader Practices to Transform Employees from Resisters to Resources for Change

Although employees can undertake any or all of the three strategies previously discussed in this chapter, leaders can help accelerate these strategies across their teams or organizations. In this section, three practices that correspond to each of the three strategies are offered to help leaders transform employees from resisters to resourceful agents of change.

Practice 1: Foster Ownership and Experimentation

Individuals who have a sense of ownership at work and are encouraged to experiment are more apt to "cut off the straps." Humans and organizations commonly share a natural tendency to preserve the status quo.[13] It is familiar and does not require an act of commission—simply doing more of the same gets us the status quo. For an employee to be empowered to be resourceful, it is important that the person feel ownership over their outcomes and have the latitude to experiment in order to optimize those outcomes. In Ethan's example of cutting off the straps, when asked why he took this rather radical action for a retail employee, he replied that the founders "always encouraged us to . . . own it and take responsibility for what we were doing, and I think that the best way they were able to get us to do that . . . is to also give us a lot of flexibility." Fostering ownership and experimentation, especially during change, might strike many as counterintuitive. During change, practitioners often divide work between strategists, who have ideas, and implementers, who simply apply those ideas. But such conventional wisdom discourages employees from being resourceful, causing leaders to miss the tremendous opportunity of mobilizing their staff to find novel ways of implementing change from a group of individuals often closest to products, services, and customers.

Practice 2: Focus on the Big Picture and Hidden Benefits

You can encourage employees to create motivational resources by taking steps that help them to understand how change is part of a larger strategy and to find the hidden benefits. During change, employees understandably worry about the costs of change, such as lost political power, changed relationships, or extra work. These are natural concerns for anyone. Human psychology leads us to focus on losses, not gains.[14] You can reorient employees by focusing on hidden benefits by helping them ask questions such as the following: What skills will you build during this change? What new relationships might you be able to forge? How will you grow as a person? By shaping the questions employees ask, you can nudge them to shift their stories of change toward benefits, and not to focus exclusively on costs.[15]

Another important way leaders can shape employee storytelling is by helping employees understand how change is part of a larger plan. This understanding is important because employees often get cynical during repeated change efforts and sometimes view managers as capricious actors proposing a "change of the month."[16] Instead of restricting information from employees, you can help employees understand the larger objective of the change. Giving employees this information will make them more apt to create the essential motivational resources to implement change in ways that help the organization, often in ways not anticipated by leaders.

Practice 3: Remind Employees of Their Capabilities . . . But Also the Urgency of the Situation

Under the traditional tale of employee resistance to change, employees often get discouraged because leaders not only write off their potential contributions to change but also label them as counterproductive for change. Reminding employees of their knowledge, experience, and values can help them interpret themselves as resources, that is, as having key capabilities making them ready and able to implement change. Ironically, a focus on the positive, without raising doubts, is likely to sideline employees who might feel good about themselves, but do not recognize the urgency of the situation. Seeding mild forms of doubt, such as gentle reminders about the severity of an organization's challenges, alongside strong reminders of the valuable resources employees possess, helps employees view themselves as important—and also motivated—contributors to change.

Putting It All Together

Looking across all three strategies and practices raises a challenge for leaders: to be resourceful themselves, in addition to helping their employees be resourceful. Leaders can "cut off the straps" in treating employees as obstacles to change, transforming what many have historically considered an obstacle into one of the most valuable resources for change. When you interpret employees in this light, it makes focusing on the big picture and hidden benefits much easier. Leaders approach change with a more open mind about employees, and interpret them as eager participants, rather than as stubborn obstacles. This approach will fundamentally reshape the story of change as a battle between strategists and implementers to one of a collective contribution across all levels of an organization. It will benefit employees, leaders, and the organization at large.

RESOURCEFUL LEADING IN THE RETAIL SECTOR

Ethan serves as an exemplar of a resourceful leader during change. In addition to "cutting off the straps" (Strategy 1), Ethan also exemplifies the other two strategies outlined in this chapter. Ethan serves as "storyteller of the big picture and benefits" (Strategy 2) when, despite the growing pains he experiences at this rapidly expanding organization, he nevertheless finds hidden benefits. He discovered having "a larger infrastructure . . . to ensure success and to ensure that we could weather some major financial disaster or some huge mistake." By storytelling the big picture, Ethan helps encourage his employees to be resourceful themselves in the service of a larger vision for change.

Finally, Ethan "integrates self-affirmation with doubt" (Strategy 3) when he creates positive meaning about his job experience while raising important doubts that generate urgency. Ethan remarks, "I'm kind of not sure if I'm . . . taking my store on the right path. . . . And that's coming from someone who's been doing this for six years." Ethan's joint acknowledgment of doubt and affirmation of experience recognizes an important humility needed when facing difficult challenge. It is a humility leaders often struggle to achieve. But it also underscores the need for Ethan to continue to be resourceful at his organization because solutions to difficult problems rarely come easily. Finally, by acknowledging his own tentativeness, Ethan is much more likely to reach out to his team to help him collectively tackle his unit's challenges, thereby turning his employees into more resourceful agents of change.

TWEETS

Employees can be resources, not resisters, to help advance change . . . only if leaders allow them.

Cut off the straps during change: enable employees to promote change by transforming the invaluable to the valuable.

Doubt during change can help create the urgency needed to successfully implement change.

13

Create Opportunity from Crisis

Lynn Perry Wooten and
Erika Hayes James

Business crises almost daily dominate the headlines, hitting the information superhighway at warp speed. Reputations are damaged, devastating both small, local companies and international conglomerates. The examples are everywhere. BP and the Deepwater Horizon oil spill. Toyota's "sticky" gas pedal recall. The Livestrong Foundation and cyclist Lance Armstrong's doping scandal. The CEO of Abercrombie & Fitch stating he was marketing only to "cool kids," and not the overweight ones. The Carnival Cruise ship stuck for days without electricity in the Gulf of Mexico. The employees of Specialty Medical Supplies kidnapping their own CEO over plans to take their jobs offshore.

The Institute for Crisis Management defines a business crisis as "any problem or disruption that triggers negative stakeholder reaction that could impact the organization's financial strength and ability to do what it does."[1] Crises are rare and significant events, challenging leaders beyond a typical "problem" because of the time pressure and the associated public scrutiny. Additional challenges for the crisis leader come from inadequate information for decision making and, in the worst cases, limited resources, including time, money, and know-how.

No matter what causes a crisis—human error, natural disaster, or controversial practices—those in leadership positions are responsible for preventing, assessing, mitigating, reacting to, resolving, and learning from a crisis. Of course, those things are hard to do in the face of sudden, urgent, and unpredictable circumstances. Regrettably, the latter step, learning from crisis, is something many leaders skip altogether.

Our work with organizations, large and small, echoes our research on leading through crisis. We have identified a way to move through crisis proactively, effectively, and with integrity through these four strategies: (1) learn, reflect, and adapt; (2) scan and see possibilities; (3) engender trust and behave authentically; and (4) embrace crisis as opportunity.

Why Care about Crisis Leadership?

If you have not (yet) faced a crisis, it may seem foolish to expend time, thought, and energy on this type of "what if." Being prepared to act, rather than just react, in the face of the unexpected can mean the difference between narrowly surviving (if you are lucky) and thriving after your organization weathers a crisis. Even mom-and-pop shops are at risk: a handful of negative local reviews on Yelp.com, a living-wage controversy with a few picketers on Main Street, or the legitimate firing of a vocal employee can attract a public spotlight so blinding that a business dies. Even the leaders in nonprofit organizations and government agencies are not shielded from crises.

Our research shows crisis leaders require more than just a step-by-step crisis management guide addressing the "during," but not the "before" or "after." Exemplary crisis leadership reaches beyond what we know of merely good leadership, exhibiting a positive leadership framework. It opens a leader's mind to handle the unexpected, as a crisis almost always is, with fresh eyes, inquisitiveness, and mindfulness, even when the precipitating event requires an almost immediate response.[2] Moreover, this framework brings a different perspective to a crisis situation, placing emphasis on elevating individuals and systems to produce extraordinary outcomes such as resilience, the ability to recover quickly, collective resourcefulness, positive interpretation, and positive relationships.[3, 4]

So why care about crisis leadership? Being a positive leader in a crisis context makes you a better leader overall, along with many other benefits. It elevates you beyond who you were before the crisis occurred, building skills, intelligence, and strength of character, as much as it elevates your organization. It becomes second nature to take actions that exemplify virtuousness by exhibiting moral goodness, human strengths, courage, resilience, and a concern for the well-being of your organization's stakeholders.[5] It also means focusing on the possibility that the crisis could generate extraordinary outcomes that change the company and its individuals for the better.[6] Being a positive leader in crisis means believing the organization can not only survive the crisis but indeed also learn to thrive because of it.

Strategy 1: Learn, Reflect, and Adapt

Are you willing and able to grow and change at any point in a process? Leaders with a learning orientation answer yes. When confronted by crisis, they (1) acknowledge the need for learning, reflection, and adapting to changing circumstances; and (2) recognize that times of crisis motivate leaders and organizations to learn, change, adapt, and innovate more than any other.[7] Remember that learning is just one part of moving through a crisis. Damage containment and recovery are equally critical, otherwise an organization can get "stuck" in learning mode and lose ground.

At the core is the ability to acquire knowledge, reflect on it, and implement a change in behavior. Leaders and their organizations can actually reduce a crisis's negative impact, so long as they are willing to examine the root causes of the crisis and value that data for decision making. Before Hurricane Katrina even hit land, Wal-Mart marshaled its extensive distribution network and data analytical systems to stock its stores with supplies for the disaster to come. Because it had learned from previous hurricanes, it served the Gulf Coast better than other companies or public institutions.[8] It learned from past crises, reflected on what worked best, and adapted its actions to fit the current event.

Learning as you go is not optimal during crisis. Instead, create opportunities for employees to learn about crisis leadership ahead of time. Let them discuss and analyze the company's vulnerabilities. Let them envision ways the organization can plan for the future and respond to stakeholders.[9] Allow discussion group members to emerge as potential crisis leaders, rather than presuming you will draw from those traditionally designated as management or senior leaders. One thing is critical: this opportunity must occur in a psychologically "safe" space, free of finger-pointing and judgment, and open to ideas and questions from all. A safe space allows for difficult conversations. It does not penalize honesty, even if this means confronting facts that are hard to hear or place the organization at risk. Even outside the confines of an in-house group, learning can occur. Encourage your team to seek and to be open to knowledge from diverse sources. This openness will allow your organization to experiment with a variety of ideas as they explore solutions for resolving a crisis.

Strategy 2: Scan and See Possibilities

Where exactly do things stand? What is the situation now? What could come of it? What are some short-term fixes? What are some longer-term solutions? These types of questions, and the means for answering them, are no different from those we face daily in business. The difference in crisis mode is everything is happening rapidly, with many unknowns despite your best knowledge-gathering efforts. Be open to external expertise from nonobvious sources and consider context and applicability to the current situation.

As you seek to learn more about the crisis, you will naturally find yourself scanning the environment and drawing conclusions from what you observe, which in turn equips you as a leader to see possible ways to resolve it.[10] "Sense-making," as this process is sometimes called, entails scanning information from multiple sources, integrating the information into a broader context, and connecting the dots at both the strategic and tactical levels. As a leader, you are most likely to take a big-picture approach, allowing the organization to recognize and to appreciate its responsibility and accountability to all stakeholders. During the scanning process, encourage discussion and debate within your organization. Invite people to challenge the status quo and explore the pathways to various possibilities. Welcome input from everyone.

Consider "scenario planning" as one part of scanning and seeing possibilities. Encourage your group to create a series of "different futures" based on scanning environmental factors such as demographics, political, economic, social, technological, legal, natural environment, and global trends that are key driving forces.[11] Scenario planning during crisis helps leaders create cognitive maps, providing a reference point from which to navigate unfamiliar terrain. As you and your colleagues scan your environment and plan scenarios, develop a mindset of "thinking about the unthinkable." You will engage in anticipatory brainstorming and learn how to consider a range of possibilities for the future that take uncertainty into account.

Declining revenues in an era of increasingly competing media led the *Detroit Free Press* newspaper to engage in scanning and identifying possibilities. To address this "smoldering" crisis, the *Detroit Free Press* worked with design company IDEO to create scenarios for the future by observing information-consuming habits of their customers at home, work, and in everyday settings. These scanning efforts guided the development of new offerings, such as changes in newspaper delivery and an expanded online presence.

Strategy 3: Engender Trust and Behave Authentically

A leader's trust and authenticity come into play in several ways during crisis. Internally, leading from a place of trust and authenticity creates a positive culture in which the goals of organizational members are aligned, and they communicate freely with good news and bad. When Alan Mulally first joined the Ford Motor Company as president and CEO, he immersed himself in all the information he could find about the company, past and present. He discussed his impressions frankly with employees. At first, they hesitated to be as open and honest as he seemed to be. But in time, they bought into the culture Mulally sought to create. A positive culture is an outgrowth of collective transcendent behaviors, including a sense of caring relating to the organization's goals, the ability to be other-focused, group efficacy, and courage.[12] As a leader, establishing trust and authenticity with your team will pay off during a crisis because team members will be honest about questions, concerns, skills, limitations, and intentions. That same trust and authenticity are critical in interacting with the stakeholders and the public in general, once crisis occurs. When stakeholders trust your brand, they trust you to fix what is broken. If they have no prior relationship with you, authentic and trustworthy behavior can quickly neutralize a negative first impression.

Strategy 4: Embrace Crisis as Opportunity

Too often, leaders focus on the negative aspects of a crisis and do not perceive the opportunities in the situation. Crises are opportunities for organizational change and revitalization because a crisis brings to leadership's attention issues that have been neglected. It also presents possibilities for innovation and system improvements.[13] This window demands that leaders transition from feelings of anger, anxiety, guilt, and despair to an outlook of optimism and hope. Perceiving a crisis as an opportunity calls leaders to embody a radical vision that inspires organizational members to identify the strengths of the organization and its environment and use them as resources. In addition, crisis situations are opportunities to rebuild and to refocus an organization's capacity.

A crisis is an opportunity to learn. If you are to be successful at embracing this opportunity, you must be willing not only to address the symptom relating to the crisis but also the root causes—to be open to whatever you discover and to encourage a climate of openness in your employees. Know that there is value in crisis, and share that knowledge with your organization before, during, and after a crisis occurs. This value can manifest in many forms, such as improved performance, enhancements to the organization's reputation, and innovations.

Putting It All Together

Crises can be opportunities for organizations to get better, to act with greater integrity, to work more efficiently, to manufacture more cleanly, to improve safety, and to treat people more fairly. Of course, when someone, such as a customer, organization, whistleblower, or rival company, points out that something is "wrong," it is hard to step up to a microphone and say thank you. Yet, the possibilities for gratitude exist. No matter how vindictive their accusations may seem at the time, these stakeholders are providing the organization with an opportunity to do better, to be better, and to achieve as never before. They are offering the organization a chance to demonstrate resilience, to adapt to its environment, to make sense of a situation, to take perspective, to be open to learning, and to build on the knowledge repository. And this is an opportunity worth taking.

FORD MOTOR COMPANY: A LESSON IN POSITIVE CRISIS LEADERSHIP

By now, everyone knows Ford endured the Great Recession of 2008 without the infamous government bailouts given to General Motors and Chrysler.[14] But Ford did not simply survive the uncertainty and devastating economic circumstances—it thrived. Ford emerged from the crisis in a better strategic position, bolstered by widespread consumer confidence and respect, including frequent recognition as one of the United

States' most trusted companies. How did Ford manage to thrive during this crisis? By seeing crisis as opportunity, Ford's top executives, CEO Alan Mulally and Chairman Bill Ford Jr., exemplified positive leadership, allowing the company to emerge as a stronger organization positioned for postrecession growth.

Strategy 1: Learn, Reflect, and Adapt

When Mulally joined Ford in 2006, he was an outsider to Detroit's auto industry. He decided to set the standard for openness and learning, with endless interest in studying the company's recent and distant past. Mulally ramped up the use of data and charts to make the company's operations more transparent to the whole executive team. A whole room filled with charts displayed the company's operational results. By modeling the skill of learning from and resolving challenges, rather than hiding them or assigning blame, Mulally and his team built a Ford culture ready to address the full force of the recession crisis.

Strategy 2: Scan and See Possibilities

Before Mulally's arrival, Ford was struggling to compete, suffering multibillion-dollar losses as the company lost market share to foreign competition. Ford Jr. had already begun assessing the economic environment, and as Mulally came on board, they agreed a recession was possible and that Ford needed to have cash on hand to survive. They leveraged many assets, including the "blue oval" brand, which initially caused doubt among creditors. When the recession hit, Ford had enough cash on hand to continue to be open to more opportunities. In fact, the two leaders recognized that investing in research and development while their competitors struggled through bankruptcy would enable them to emerge from the crisis in a strong strategic position. As they analyzed their situation, they invested in key development areas, including lighter and more fuel-efficient cars, to gain a competitive advantage.

Strategy 3: Engender Trust and Behave Authentically

Building a positive culture in which team members are aligned and communicating openly—both good news and bad—is crucial to leading with trust and authenticity. For his part, Mulally wanted to avoid being blindsided by covered-up issues. So he developed a concept, which he called "One Ford," that emphasized the point that they were all on one team. When he recognized trust was missing among the executive team, he worked to align executives' interests and goals by changing incentive structures to account for company-wide performance. He modeled the behavior of being open and transparent about challenges and vulnerabilities by asking for everyone to help solve a problem, even if the problem fell largely under one executive's jurisdiction. Any problem was everyone's problem, he said, and it was not just the fault of the one executive responsible for that area. By facilitating a positive culture of collaboration and open communication among the "One Ford" team, he ensured issues were dealt with proactively before they became company-wide.

Externally, Ford built trust through their dedication to avoiding bankruptcy and federal bailout dollars. As Ford proved it could navigate the recession without taxpayer money, customers took note. Multiple polls showed people were more likely to buy a Ford product solely because the company did not take taxpayer loans. Instead, small-business owners and consumers alike sent letters praising company leaders for refusing the money and managing their business wisely. Customers did not have to question whether to buy a car from a bankrupt company. Ford was solvent. Since the recession, Ford has been ranked one of the top ten trusted brands by YouGov's BrandIndex.[15]

Strategy 4: Embrace Crisis as Opportunity

As the recession hit, Ford leadership recognized the opportunity to become more efficient and to develop their internal business processes to position them well for the future. By accelerating the development of new products, such as fuel-efficient vehicles, and aggressively restructuring to improve its operating efficiency, Ford took advantage of the chance to learn and to adapt rather than simply hunkering down and trying to survive. They reduced redundancies by building more cars using the same platforms, rather than letting each division and brand operate independently; in addition to aligning with Mulally's "One Ford" vision, this move allowed Ford to gain savings that would last beyond the crisis. In addition, Ford continued to focus on discovering new ideas to position itself strategically for the future, partnering with university researchers to develop important technologies for the next generation of smaller, lighter cars.

When the recession hit, many loud voices were saying the era of U.S. manufacturing was over, and that it was time to let the Big Three die. Given the economic crisis, this attitude could have swayed many leaders; instead, Mulally believed in and looked for opportunities before and during the recession. He built trust and showed a willingness to learn as the crisis evolved. Ford leadership stands as a shining example that, operating within a positive leadership framework, crises can become opportunities for an organization to grow and to thrive.

TWEETS

Not if—but when—business crisis hits: become a student. See crisis as an opportunity to learn.

In crisis leadership: figure out how to change and to improve your business, not just bounce back.

Four strategies for positive crisis leadership: learn and reflect, scan for possibilities and plan, gain trust, and embrace crisis as opportunity.

Epilogue and Looking Forward

*Gretchen M. Spreitzer and
Jane E. Dutton*

This book brings together respected thought leaders in positive organizational scholarship (POS) to share their best bets on how to become a positive leader. Each bet, or what we term a seed, is backed by scientific evidence and brought to life through stories of real organizations or leaders using these seeds. This collection of seeds reveals the different ways POS opens up new lines of sight for leaders to engage in practices fostering expanding possibilities for excellence.[1] These new lines of sight are critical, yet often dismissed, as "soft" and "inconsequential." Nothing could be further from the truth, as new lines of sight are critical. They help generate new possibilities for bringing out the best in people and in systems, and for changing trajectories for excellence in the future.

Let us make the potential impact of positive leadership more concrete. Consider the impact of positive leadership in a large organization undergoing a significant change. This organization has a history of being bureaucratic, but also of taking care of its people. With a mandate to do more with less and an external environment of scarcity, the organization aimed to enhance efficiency and reduce costs by centralizing certain organizational functions. This mandate would not only relocate some employees to different parts of the organization, it would also eliminate employees in a setting where large-scale layoffs were quite uncommon. E-mails were sent throughout the organization, explaining the change. Senior leadership sought to do no harm in implementing the change to create a more efficient structure. Because the organization was large, the communication plans called for using mass e-mails to describe the changes in the organization's structure and the elimination of employee positions. The initial e-mail introducing these changes to the community was scheduled for a Friday evening delivery, which provided no time for processing what it meant before the weekend. The tone of these e-mails was carefully descriptive of the changes, but did not provide any detail about services available to affected employees. However, leaders in one of the organization's units deployed a distinctly different approach that employed several positive leadership practices.

Leaders in the "deviant" unit articulated overarching goals for the change, including creating a supportive environment for everyone affected by the change. They used the change as an opportunity to perform the work of the organization more effectively, not only more efficiently; to strengthen connections between people; and to cultivate pride in the organization during the process. These overarching goals helped shape and guide conversations at all levels, providing a focus on the benefits to be gained from the change rather than on the inherent losses. The change process used extensive face-to-face communication, building higher-quality connections between all members of the unit. E-mails were only relied upon to announce meetings and indicate, in a general way, that the unit was going to take a different approach to implementing change. These communication moves worked, fostering respect and trust, enabling work performance during the change. Unit leaders also engaged in a continuous process of seeking solutions from the employees themselves, treating them as resources— not resisters—even though several employees' jobs could be eliminated. Leaders at multiple levels encouraged employees to provide input about ways to craft and to rearrange their work to foster collaboration and fully use people's strengths. Unit members began to think of themselves as a group, filled with competent and caring individuals, and people worked toward this positive identity.

Leaders sought to cultivate hope and reconnect members to the organization's higher purpose, emphasizing the organization's contributions to society and affirming each employee's role in making this purpose a reality. Through this composite of positive leader strategies, people throughout the unit saw new potential and strengths in the individuals and in the system. The quality of the relationships between people improved, building capacity for future collaboration, trust, and engagement. Energy levels expanded, rather than contracted, and people reported learning and growing despite the press for organizational contraction. Innovative solutions emerged, through new pools for accessing talent and new processes for providing career services. Leaders saw their individual and organizational capacities for excellence expand in a few short weeks. Not only was a crisis averted, but as one employee said, "We used this crisis as an opportunity to become a better version of ourselves." Taking this route meant respectfully deviating from the master organizational plan while maintaining good relationships with the individuals who constructed the plan. The positive leader made it a priority to still function effectively within the larger environment while implementing the change with a different set of practices.

Core Insights about Positive Leadership

Positive leaders understand there are always relationships to strengthen, resources to unlock, good to tap, and change processes to engage that enhance, rather than diminish, future possibilities for excellence. Positive leaders know that seemingly small actions, such as connecting employees to the beneficiaries of their work (Grant, "Outsource Inspiration," this volume), fostering employees' capacity to see themselves as growing at work (Roberts, "Cultivate Positive Identities," this volume), acting as if the future looks bright (Branzei, "Cultivate Hope," this volume), encouraging employees to be resourceful in change (Sonenshein, "Treat Employees as Resources," this volume), or expressing more gratitude to others (Cameron, "Activate Virtuousness," this volume) can unleash new possibilities. Positive leaders are engaged in actions—it is leadership in motion, not leadership standing still. Single small actions can have multiple beneficial effects.

Positive leaders expand the zone of possibility for excellence in individuals, teams, and organizations by treating meaning, relationships, vision, initiative, and virtues as sources of strength and enhanced capacity. Being a positive leader means taking action from a place of grounded optimism. It means knowing there are solid reasons to believe that greater levels of excellence are possible, even when material and financial resources are limited. A positive leadership approach demonstrates how small actions carry psychological and relational potencies that are deeply impactful and sustainable over time.

Positive leaders do not see people, teams, or organizations as limited entities with fixed capacities. Instead, they see and act on abundant possibilities for expansion and renewal of vital resources inside people, relationships, and teams. Optimism, hope, gratitude, joy, excitement, energy, efficacy, flexibility, respect, trust, and support are the fuel and engine of improved capacities for excellence. Positive leaders appreciate the expansion of possibilities enabled by contagion and the spread of emotions, ideas, and connections that affect the speed and extent to which capacities for excellence can be enlarged. Returning to Figure 1 we introduced in the Invitation introduction, positive leaders expand the zone of possibility, allowing individuals, units, or whole organizations to alter the rate and the level of possible excellence. One question you may be asking is how to get started on your own journey to becoming a positive leader.

Five Core Nuggets for Becoming a More Positive Leader

As we looked across the chapters in the book, five core nuggets became clear. We describe each nugget below and offer an opportunity to jump-start their use in your own leadership practice.

1. Find and Cultivate Positive Meaning in Your Work and in the Work of Others

Positive meaning is a central engine for enhancing individual or collective capacity for excellence. Meaning is potent and pervasive: it is often created through the experience of work, not given or fixed. Leaders have many options to find and to cultivate meaning that strengthens or expands capacities. Meaning is a resource, unlocked through job-crafting activities (Wrzesniewski, "Engage in Job Crafting," this volume) and construction of positive identities (Roberts, "Cultivate Positive Identities," this volume). Motivation is enhanced when positive meaning is created, connecting people's work to its impact on end users or work beneficiaries (Grant, "Outsource Inspiration," this volume). Positive meaning is a consequence of finding higher purpose in one's own work or the organization's (Quinn and Thakor, "Imbue the Organization with a Higher Purpose," this volume). Reflect on the different ways that you derive positive meaning from your work or by being a part of your organization. Then consider ways you could cultivate more positive meaning into your work.

APPLICATIONS

1. I find positive meaning in my work (or job) or my organization in the following ways:

2. How could I craft my work (or job) to be more meaningful?

3. How could I think about my organization in ways that make it more meaningful to me or others?

_____

_____

_____

_____

_____

_____

_____

2. Create a Vision That Inspires You and Others around You

Vision is a well-worn term in the realm of leadership. The thought leaders in this book suggest new ways to consider vision. Imagine what could be possible, and question taken-for-granted assumptions of how things are done (Golden-Biddle, "Create Micro-moves for Organizational Change," this volume). Envision a future with hope that enables leaders to press on and go boldly forward (Branzei, "Cultivate Hope," this volume). Be open to the idea that a crisis may enable the organization to change for the better (Wooten and James, "Create Opportunity from Crisis," this volume). Sometimes vision can be created from the bottom up, rather than from the top down. Draw on the ideas of your people, no matter where they are in the organization (Sonenshein, "Treat Employees as Resources," this volume).

APPLICATIONS

1. The current vision for our unit or organization is:

_____

_____

_____

_____

_____

_____

_____

2. How could I envision a future that is more inspiring to me
   and to others?

_____

_____

_____

_____

_____

_____

3. How can I infuse the vision with greater hope?

_____

_____

_____

_____

_____

_____

3. Develop and Facilitate More High-Quality Connections for Yourself and for Others

Building and accessing high-quality connections is a critical foundation for enhancing capacities for excellence. High-quality connections provide a safe space for people to experiment and grow (Spreitzer and Porath, "Enable Thriving at Work," this volume). At the core of this strategy is the knowledge that having high-quality connections builds physiological, psychological, and social strengths for the people in them (Dutton, "Build

High-Quality Connections," this volume). Use successful pathways for facilitating high-quality connections, such as task enabling, respectful engagement, trusting, and playing (Dutton). Build high-quality connections as a means for job crafting, playing to your strengths, values, or passions (Wrzesniewski, "Engage in Job Crafting," this volume). Given the potentially conflicting nature of negotiations, be mindful about emotional triggers. Allow emotions to facilitate, rather than disrupt, high-quality connections (Kopelman and Mahalingam, "Negotiate Mindfully," this volume).

APPLICATIONS

1. How can I access or foster the creation of more high-quality connections each day?

_____

_____

_____

_____

_____

_____

_____

2. How can I access or foster the creation of more high-quality connections for people in my organization?

_____

_____

_____

_____

_____

3. How can I access and foster more high-quality connections with suppliers, customers, and other groups that are inter-dependent with my organization?

4. Be Proactive and Look for Ways for You and Others to Take Initiative

Positive leaders seek out ways to break from routines and learn new action patterns. Pair something unfamiliar with something familiar to create something new (Golden-Biddle). Seek out opportunities to learn new things and grow (Spreitzer and Porath, "Enable Thriving at Work," this volume). Take even the smallest of steps, as "if the future were guaranteed," to keep hope alive (Branzei, "Cultivate Hope," this volume). Empower employees by thinking of them as resources, able to generate new ideas and innovations (Sonenshein, "Treat Employees as Resources," this volume). Free employees to make their own decisions, reinterpreting their roles and resources in the face of formidable challenges (Sonenshein). Rather than directing, explore the unfamiliar and new possibilities together (Golden-Biddle, "Create Micro-moves for Organizational Change," this volume). By providing more decision-making discretion, help your employees thrive (Spreitzer and Porath, "Enable Thriving at Work," this volume).

APPLICATIONS

1. I tend to be proactive and take initiative in the following ways:

_____

_____

_____

_____

_____

_____

_____

2. People in my unit feel empowered to take action in the following ways:

_____

_____

_____

_____

_____

_____

3. Where is there more potential for deeper levels of leader and employee empowerment?

_____

_____

_____

_____

_____

_____

5. Make Virtuous Action a Priority

Positive leaders activate virtuousness by doing the right thing, even when it is not the easy or expected way to behave (Cameron, "Activate Virtuousness," this volume). They value character and prioritize humanity in decision making. Positive leaders model ethical behavior in their actions; they do not send mixed signals (Mayer, "Lead an Ethical Organization," this volume). They walk the talk (Mayer). Positive leaders aspire for something bigger—a life of higher purpose and virtue (Cameron, "Activate Virtuousness," this volume) and an organization with a higher purpose (Quinn and Thakor, "Imbue the Organization with a Higher Purpose," this volume).

APPLICATIONS

1. A time when I behaved in alignment with my values was:

_____

_____

_____

_____

_____

_____

_____

2. How can I facilitate more alignment of my actions with my values?

_____

_____

_____

_____

_____

_____

_____

3. As an organization, how have we acted virtuously? How can we be more virtuous in our everyday actions going forward?

_____

_____

_____

_____

_____

_____

Making Positive Leadership Stick

As a positive leader, your intentions and actions will have longer-lasting impacts if they become part of the way of "being" and "doing" in your organization. In many of this book's examples, this way of being has become part of the soil or fabric of the organization, extending benefits into the future. The positive leader's impacts are more likely to last if the organization's culture (shared values, beliefs, and norms), rewards (formal and informal), routines (selection, socialization, talent management, communication), and structures (reporting and project management systems, department or unit groupings) support the kinds of positive leader strategies that have been identified in this volume.

Being a positive leader means acting on your authentic beliefs that the situation can improve, capability can be enhanced, and better is always possible. A positive leader is not naïve, but is wise. He or she knows options are expandable by taking the human-based possibilities for greatness seriously and acting to ignite and enable them. Through the small actions identified in this book, we are confident your impact will be great.

Notes

1. Build High-Quality Connections

1. B. Fredrickson, *Love 2.0: How Our Supreme Emotion Affects Everything We Feel, Think, Do and Become* (New York: Hudson Street Press, 2013).

2. C. D. Ryff and B. H. Singer, eds., *Emotion, Social Relationships and Health* (New York: Oxford University Press, 2001).

3. E. Heaphy and J. E. Dutton, "Positive Social Interactions at Work: Linking Organizations and Physiology," *Academy of Management Review* 33, no. 1 (2008): 137–62.

4. O. Ybarra, E. Burnstein, P. Winkielman, M. C. Keller, M. Manis, E. Chan, and J. Rodriquez, "Mental Exercising through Simple Socializing: Social Interaction Promotes General Cognitive Functioning," *Personality and Social Psychology Bulletin* 34, no. 2 (2008): 248–59.

5. Fredrickson, *Love 2.0*.

6. A. Carmeli, D. Brueller, and J. E. Dutton, "Learning Behaviours in the Workplace: The Role of High-Quality Interpersonal Relationships and Psychological Safety," *Systems Research and Behavioral Science* 26, no. 1 (2009): 81–98.

7. J. P. Stephens, A. Carmeli, E. Heaphy, G. M. Spreitzer, and J. E. Dutton, "Relationship Quality and Virtuousness: Emotional Carrying Capacity as a Source of Individual and Team Resilience," *Journal of Applied Behavioral Science* 49, no. 1 (2003): 13–41.

8. D. S. Chiaburu and D. A. Harrison, "Do Peers Make the Place? Conceptual Synthesis and Meta-Analysis of Co-worker Effects on Perceptions, Attitudes, OCBs and Performance," *Journal of Applied Psychology* 93, no. 5 (2008): 1082–1103.

9. A. Carmeli and J. E. Dutton, "Linking Respectful Engagement, Relational Information Processing, and Creativity among Employees and Teams" (unpublished manuscript, 2012).

10. J. LaBianca, E. Umphress, and J. Kaufmann, "A Preliminary Test of Negative Asymmetry Hypothesis in Workplace Social Networks" (paper presented at the National Academy of Management meetings, Toronto, 2000).

11. J. H. Gittell, "A Theory of Relational Coordination," in K. Cameron, J. E. Dutton, and R. E. Quinn, eds., *Positive Organizational Scholarship: Foundations of a New Discipline* (San Francisco: Berrett-Koehler, 2003), 25–27.

12. Builds from J. E. Dutton, *Energize Your Workplace: Building High-Quality Connections at Work* (San Francisco: Jossey-Bass, 2003); J. E. Dutton and E. Heaphy, "The Power of High-Quality Connections," in K. Cameron, J. E. Dutton, and R. E. Quinn, *Positive Organizational Scholarship*, 263–78 (San Francisco: Berrett-Koehler, 2003); J. P. Stephens, E. Heaphy, and J. E. Dutton, "High-Quality Connections," in K. Cameron and G. M. Spreitzer, eds., *Handbook of Positive Organizational Scholarship* (New York: Oxford University Press, 2011).

13. C. Rogers and R. E. Farson, "Active Listening," in *Organizational Psychology*, 3rd ed. (Englewood Cliffs, NJ: Prentice Hall, 1979).

14. D. Whetten and K. Cameron, *Developing Management Skills*, 4th ed. (Reading, MA: Addison-Wesley, 1999).

15. M. B. Rosenberg, *Nonviolent Communication: A Language of Life* (Encinitas, CA: PuddleDancer Press, 2000).

16. E.g., C. Mainemelis and S. Ronson, "Ideas Are Born in Fields of Play: Towards a Theory of Play and Creativity in Organizational Settings," *Research in Organizational Behavior* 27 (2006): 81–131.

17. W. Baker and J. E. Dutton, "Enabling Positive Social Capital," in J. E. Dutton and B. Ragins, eds., *Exploring Positive Relationships at Work: Building a Theoretical and Research Foundation* (Mahwah, NJ: Lawrence Erlbaum, 2007).

18. R. Cross and A. Parker, *The Hidden Power of Networks* (Boston: Harvard Business School Press, 2004).

19. J. H. Gittell, *The Southwest Airlines Way: Using the Power of Relationships to Achieve High Performance* (New York: McGraw-Hill, 2003).

20. K. Rollag, R. Cross, and S. Parise, "Getting New Hires up to Speed Quickly," *MIT Sloan Management Review* 46, no. 2 (2005): 35–41.

21. M. Harrington, *Embodied Care: Jane Addams, Maurice Merleau-Ponty and Feminist Ethics* (Chicago: University of Illinois Press, 2004); S. Simola, "Exploring 'Embodied Care' in Relation to Social Sustainability," *Journal of Business Ethics* 107 (2012): 473–84.

22. J. E. Dutton, P. Frost, M. Worline, J. Lilius, and J. Kanov, "Leading in Times of Trauma," *Harvard Business Review* (January 2002): 54–61.

2. Outsource Inspiration

1. B. D. Rosso, K. H. Dekas, and A. Wrzesniewski, "On the Meaning of Work: A Theoretical Integration and Review," *Research in Organizational Behavior* 30 (2010): 91–127.

2. J. R. Hackman and G. R. Oldham, "Motivation through the Design of Work: Test of a Theory," *Organizational Behavior and Human Performance* 16, no. 2 (1976): 250–79.

3. A. M. Grant, E. M. Campbell, G. Chen, K. Cottone, D. Lapedis, and K. Lee, "Impact and the Art of Motivation Maintenance: The Effects of Contact with Beneficiaries on Persistence Behavior," *Organizational Behavior and Human Decision Processes* 103, no. 1 (2007): 53–67.

4. A. M. Grant, "Employees without a Cause: The Motivational Effects of Prosocial Impact in Public Service," *International Public Management Journal* 11, no. 1 (2008): 48–66.

5. A. M. Grant and D. A. Hofmann, "Outsourcing Inspiration: The Performance Effects of Ideological Messages from Leaders and Beneficiaries," *Organizational Behavior and Human Decision Processes* 116, no. 2 (2011): 173–87.

6. A. M. Grant, "The Significance of Task Significance: Job Performance Effects, Relational Mechanisms, and Boundary Conditions," *Journal of Applied Psychology* 93, no. 1 (2008): 108–24.

7. N. Belle, "Experimental Evidence on the Relationship between Public Service Motivation and Job Performance," *Public Administration Review* 73, no. 1 (2013): 143–53.

8. Y. N. Turner, I. Hadas-Halperin, and D. Raveh, *Patient Photos Spur Radiologist Empathy and Eye for Detail* (paper presented at the annual meeting of the Radiological Society of North America, Chicago, November 2008).

9. A. M. Grant, "Significance of Task Significance."

10. A. M. Grant and D. A. Hofmann, "It's Not All about Me: Motivating Hospital Hand Hygiene by Focusing on Patients," *Psychological Science* 22, no. 12 (2011): 1494–99.

11. J. Birkinshaw and S. Caulkin, "The Open Secret to Motivating Employees," *Fortune*, June 14, 2011, http://management.fortune.cnn.com/2011 /06/14/the-open-secrets-of-employee-motivation.

12. Grant et al., "Impact and Art of Motivation Maintenance;" Grant and Hofmann, "Outsourcing Inspiration."

13. B. George, *Authentic Leadership: Rediscovering the Secrets to Creating Lasting Value* (San Francisco: Jossey-Bass, 2003).

14. D. Patnaik, "Innovation Starts with Empathy: The Importance of Developing Deep Connections with the People You Serve," *Financial Times Press*, October 28, 2009, www.ftpress.com/articles/article.aspx?p=1399911& seqNum=4.

15. R. W. Boss, "Team Building and the Problem of Regression: The Personal Management Interview as an Intervention," *Journal of Applied Behavioral Science* 19, no. 1 (1983): 67–83.

16. R. W. Boss, "Just between You and the Boss," *Training and Development Journal* (November 1985): 68–71.

17. A. M. Grant and J. E. Dutton, "Beneficiary or Benefactor: Are People More Prosocial When They Reflect on Receiving or Giving?" *Psychological Science* 23, no. 9 (2012): 1033–39.

18. S. Sonnentag and A. M. Grant, "Doing Good at Work Feels Good at Home, but Not Right Away: When and Why Perceived Prosocial Impact Predicts Positive Affect," *Personnel Psychology* 65, no. 3 (2012): 495–530.

19. S. Lyubomirsky, K. Sheldon, and D. Schkade, "Pursuing Happiness: The Architecture of Sustainable Change," *Review of General Psychology* 9, no. 2 (2005): 111–31.

20. A. M. Grant, "How Customers Can Rally Your Troops: End Users Can Energize Your Workforce Far Better Than Your Managers Can," *Harvard Business Review* (June 2011): 97–103.

21. Grant, "How Customers Can Rally"; George, *Authentic Leadership*.

22. D. Katz and R. L. Kahn, *The Social Psychology of Organizations* (New York: Wiley, 1966).

23. N. Belle, "Leading to Make a Difference: A Field Experiment on the Performance Effects of Transformational Leadership, Perceived Social Impact, and Public Service Motivation," *Journal of Public Administration Research and Theory* (June 2013): 1–28.

24. A. M. Grant, "Leading with Meaning: Beneficiary Contact, Prosocial Impact, and the Performance Effects of Transformational Leadership," *Academy of Management Journal* 55, no. 2 (2012): 458–76.

25. A. M. Grant, *Give and Take: A Revolutionary Approach to Success* (New York: Viking, 2013).

3. Negotiate Mindfully

1. S. Kopelman, O. Avi-Yonah, and A. K. Varghese, "The Mindful Negotiator: Strategic Emotion Management and Well-Being," in K. Cameron and

G. M. Spreitzer, eds., *The Oxford Handbook of Positive Organizational Scholarship* (New York: Oxford University Press, 2012) 591–600.

2. S. Kopelman, A. S. Rosette, and L. Thompson, "The Three Faces of Eve: Strategic Displays of Positive, Negative, and Neutral Emotions in Negotiations," *Organizational Behavior and Human Decision Processes* 99 (2006): 81–101; S. Kopelman and A. S. Rosette, "Cultural Variation in Response to Strategic Display of Emotions During Negotiations," special issue on Emotions in Negotiation, *Group Decision and Negotiations* 17, no. 1 (2008): 65–77; S. Kopelman, I. Gewurz, and V. Sacharin, "The Power of Presence: Strategic Responses to Displayed Emotions in Negotiation," in N. M. Ashkanasy and C. L. Cooper, eds., *Research Companion to Emotions in Organizations*, 405–17 (Northampton, MA: Edward Elgar, 2008).

3. L. Thompson and R. Hastie, "Social Perception in Negotiation," *Organization Behavior and Human Decision Processes* 47, no. 1 (1990): 98–123.

4. D. A. Lax and J. K. Sebenius, *The Manager as Negotiator: Bargaining for Cooperation and Competitive Gain* (New York: Free Press, 1986); D. G. Pruitt and J. Z. Rubin, *Social Conflict: Escalation, Stalemate and Settlement* (New York: Random House, 1986); H. Raiffa, *The Art and Science of Negotiation* (Cambridge, MA: Harvard University Press, 1982).

5. For a review, see R. J. Lewicki, D. Saunders, and B. Barry, *Negotiation* (Boston: McGraw-Hill/Irwin, 2009); L. Thompson, *The Mind and Heart of the Negotiator*, 5th ed. (Upper Saddle River, NJ: Prentice Hall, 2012); M. Bazerman and M. Neale, *Negotiating Rationally* (New York: Free Press, 1992).

6. S. Kopelman, R. Mahalingam, and I. Gewurz, "Mindfully Managing Emotions and Resolving Paradoxes in the Context of Negotiations," in M. Benoliel, *Negotiation Excellence: Successful Deal Making* (Singapore: World Scientific, 2014).

7. S. J. Ashford and D. S. DeRue, "Developing as a Leader: The Power of Mindful Engagement," *Organizational Dynamics* 41, no. 2 (2013): 146–54; R. A. Baer, E. Walsh, and E. Lykins, "Assessment of Mindfulness," in F. Didonna, ed., *Clinical Handbook of Mindfulness*, 153–68 (New York: Springer, 2009); K. W. Brown and R. M. Ryan, "Perils and Promise in Defining and Measuring Mindfulness: Observations from Experience," *Clinical Psychology: Science and Practice* 11, no. 3 (2004); K. E. Weick, K. M. Sutcliffe, and D. Obstefeld, "Organizing High Reliability: Processes of Collective Mindfulness," in R. Sutton and B. Staw, eds., *Research in Organizational Behavior*, 81–124 (Greenwich, CT: JAI Press, 1999).

8. S. Kopelman, *Negotiating Genuinely: Being Yourself in Business* (Stanford, CA: Stanford University Press, forthcoming 2014); Kopelman et al., "Mindful Negotiator."

9. P. Gilbert and D. Tirch, "Emotional Memory: Mindfulness and Compassion," in F. Didonna, ed., *Clinical Handbook of Mindfulness*, 99–110 (New York: Springer, 2009).

10. C. McDonald, *Awakening the Kind Heart: How to Meditate on Compassion* (Somerville, MA: Wisdom, 2010); Y. Cohen-Charash, M. Erez, and C. A. Scherbaum, "When good things happen to others: Envy and firgun reactions" (symposium, Society for Industrial and Organizational Psychology, San Francisco, CA, April 2008).

11. B. L. Fredrickson, M. A. Cohn, K. A. Coffey, J. Pek, and S. M. Finkel, "Open Hearts Build Lives: Positive Emotions, Induced through Loving-Kindness Meditation, Build Consequential Personal Resources," *Journal of Personality and Social Psychology* 95 (2008): 1045–62.

12. J. Kanov, S. Maitlis, M. Worline, J. E. Dutton, P. Frost, and J. Lilius, "Compassion in Organizational Life," *American Behavioral Scientist* 47, no. 6 (2004), 808–27; J. E. Dutton and K. M. Workman, "Compassion as a Generative Force," *Journal of Management Inquiry* 20 (2012): 401–6; J. E. Dutton, M. Worline, P. Frost, and J. Lilius, "Explaining Compassion Organizing," *Administrative Science Quarterly* 51, no. 1 (2006): 59–96.

13. S. Kopelman, J. Shoshana, and L. Chen, "Re-narrating Positive Relational Identities in Organizations: Self-Narration as a Mechanism for Strategic Emotion Management in Interpersonal Interactions" in L. M. Roberts and J. E. Dutton, eds., *Exploring Positive Identities and Organizations: Building a Theoretical and Research Foundation*, 265–87 (New York: Taylor & Francis Group, 2009); Kopelman et al., "Mindful Negotiator."

14. J. J. Gross and R. A. Thompson, "Emotion Regulation: Conceptual Foundations," in J. J. Gross, ed., *Handbook of Emotion Regulation*, 3–24 (New York: Guilford Press, 2007).

15. Kopelman et al., "The Three Faces of Eve."

16. Kopelman, *Negotiating Genuinely*; Kopelman et al., "Mindful Negotiator."

17. Amos, personal interview by S. Kopelman, October 2013; Rina Petilon, "Urban Legend," September 12, 2009, http://www.rest.co.il/article.aspx?articleID=4787.

4. Enable Thriving at Work

1. G. M. Spreitzer, K. Sutcliffe, J. E. Dutton, S. Sonenshein, and A. Grant, "A Socially Embedded Model of Thriving at Work," *Organization Science* 16, no. 5 (2005): 537–49.

2. C. Porath, G. M. Spreitzer, C. Gibson, and F. Garnett, "Thriving at Work: Toward Its Measurement, Construct Validation, and Theoretical Refinement," *Journal of Organizational Behavior* 33, no. 2 (2012): 250–71.

3. R. Quinn, G. M. Spreitzer, and C. F. Lam, "A Comprehensive Review and Integrative Framework of Energy at Work," *Academy of Management Annals* (2012): 337–96.

4. G. M. Spreitzer and C. Porath, "Creating Sustainable Performance," *Harvard Business Review,* January–February (2012): 92–99.

5. Porath et al., "Thriving at Work," 250–71.

6. Quinn, Spreitzer, and Lam, "Comprehensive Review and Integrative Framework," 337–96.

7. G. M. Spreitzer et al., "Socially Embedded Model of Thriving," 537–49.

8. M. Ford and P. Smith, "Thriving with Social Purpose: An Integrative Approach to the Development of Optimal Human Functioning," *Educational Psychologist* 42, no. 3 (2007): 153–71.

9. G. M. Spreitzer, "Psychological Empowerment in the Workplace: Dimensions, Measurement, and Validation," *Academy of Management Journal* 38, no. 5 (1995): 1442–65.

10. C. Niessen, S. Sonnentag, and F. Sach, "Thriving at Work: A Diary Study," *Journal of Organizational Behavior* 33 (2012): 468–87.

11. C. Fritz, C. F. Lam, and G. M. Spreitzer, "It's the Little Things That Matter: An Examination of Knowledge Workers' Energy Management," *Academy of Management Perspectives* 25, no. 3 (2011): 28–39.

12. E. L. Deci and R. M. Ryan, *Handbook of Self-Determination Research* (Rochester, NY: University of Rochester Press, 2002).

13. S. J. Ashford and D. S. DeRue, "Developing as a Leader: The Power of Mindful Engagement," *Organizational Dynamics* 41, no. 2 (2012): 146–54.

14. A. Parker, A. Gerbasi, and C. L. Porath, "The Effects of De-Energizing Ties in Organizations and How to Manage Them," *Organizational Dynamics* 42 (2013): 110–18.

15. J. Loehr and T. Schwartz, *The Power of Full Engagement: Managing Energy, Not Time, Is the Key to High Performance and Renewal* (New York: Free Press, 2003).

16. G. M. Spreitzer and T. Grant, "Helping Students Manage Their Energy: Taking Their Pulse with the Energy Audit," *Journal of Management Education* 36, no. 2 (2012): 239–63.

17. C. Pearson and C. Porath, *The Cost of Bad Behavior—How Incivility Damages Your Business and What You Can Do about It* (New York: Penguin Group Inc., 2009).

18. C. Porath and C. Pearson, "The Price of Incivility: Lack of Respect in the Workplace Hurts Morale—and the Bottom Line," *Harvard Business Review*, January–February (2013).

19. K. De Stobbeleir and S. Ashford, "Feedback-Seeking Behavior in Organizations: Research, Theory and Implications," in R. M. Sutton,

M. J. Hornsey, and K. M. Douglas, eds., *Feedback: The Communication of Praise, Criticism, and Advice* (New York: Peter Lang International Academic Publishers, 2012).

20. W. Baker, "Openbook Finance at Zingerman's," GlobaLens Case 1-429-091, October 2010.

5. Cultivate Positive Identities

1. J. E. Dutton, L. M. Roberts, and J. Bednar, "Pathways for Positive Identity Construction at Work: Four Types of Positive Identity and the Building of Social Resources," *Academy of Management Review* 35 (2010): 265–93.

2. L. Hill and K. Lineback, *Being the Boss: The 3 Imperatives for Becoming a Great Leader* (Boston: Harvard Business Review Press, 2011).

3. A. Grant, J. E. Dutton, and B. Rosso, "Giving Commitment: Employee Support Programs and the Prosocial Sensemaking Process," *Academy of Management Journal* 51 (2008): 898–918.

4. C. Bartel, "Social Comparisons in Boundary-Spanning Work: Effects of Community Outreach on Members' Organizational Identity and Identification," *Administrative Science Quarterly* 46 (2001): 379–414.

5. S. Maitlis, "Who Am I Now? Sensemaking and Identity in Posttraumatic Growth," in L. M. Roberts and J. E. Dutton, eds., *Exploring Positive Identities and Organizations: Building a Theoretical and Research Foundation*, 47–76 (New York: Routledge, 2009); S. Sonenshein, J. E. Dutton, A. Grant, G. M. Spreitzer, and K. Sutcliffe, "Growing at Work: Employees' Interpretations of Progressive Self-Change in Organizations," *Organization Science* (forthcoming).

6. C. Cheng, J. Sanchez-Burks, and F. Lee, "Connecting the Dots Within: Creative Performance and Identity Integration," *Psychological Science* 19 (2008): 1178–84; B. Caza and M. Wilson, "Me, Myself, and I: The Benefits of Work-Identity Complexity," in L. M. Roberts and J. E. Dutton, eds., *Exploring Positive Identities and Organizations: Building a Theoretical and Research Foundation*, 99–123 (New York: Routledge, 2009).

7. D. A. Thomas, "Diversity as Strategy," *Harvard Business Review* 82, no. 9 (2004): 98–108.

8. B. Ashforth, G. Kreiner, M. Clark, and M. Fugate, "Normalizing Dirty Work: Managerial Tactics for Countering Occupational Taint," *Academy of Management Journal* 50 (2007): 149–74.

9. A. Wrzesniewski and J. E. Dutton, "Having a Calling and Crafting a Job: The Case of Candice Billups" (video), GlobaLens Case 1-428-883, November 2009.

10. R. S. Burt, "The Social Structure of Competition," in N. Nohria and R. Eccles, eds., *Networks and Organizations: Structure, Form, and Action*, 57–91 (Boston: Harvard Business School Press, 1992).

11. S. DeRue and S. Ashford, "Who Will Lead and Who Will Follow? A Social Process of Leadership Identity Construction in Organizations," *Academy of Management Review* 35, no. 4 (2010): 627–47.

12. B. Owens and D. Hekman, "Modeling to Grow: An Inductive Examination of Humble Leader Behaviors, Contingencies, and Outcomes," *Academy of Management Journal* 55, no. 4 (2012): 787–818; R. Ely and D. Meyerson, "An Organizational Approach to Undoing Gender: The Unlikely Case of Offshore Oil Platforms," *Research in Organizational Behavior* 30 (2010): 3–34.

13. C. J. Bryan, G. S. Adams, and B. Monin, "When Cheating Would Make You a Cheater: Implicating the Self Prevents Unethical Behavior," *Journal of Experimental Psychology: General* 142, no. 4 (2013): 1001–5.

14. C. Peterson and M. Seligman, *Character Strengths and Virtues: A Handbook and Classification* (Washington, DC: American Psychological Association, 2004).

15. J. E. Dutton, L. M. Roberts, and J. Bednar, "Prosocial Practices, Positive Identity, and Flourishing at Work," in S. Donaldson, M. Csikszentmihalyi, and J. Nakamura, eds., *Applied Positive Psychology: Improving Everyday Life, Schools, Work, Health, and Society*, 155–70 (New York: Taylor & Francis, 2011).

16. K. Sheldon and S. Lyubormirski, "How to Increase and Sustain Positive Emotion: The Effects of Expressing Gratitude and Visualizing Best Possible Selves," *Journal of Positive Psychology* 1 (2006): 73–82.

17. H. Ibarra, "Provisional Selves: Experimenting with Image and Identity in Professional Adaptation," *Administrative Science Quarterly* 44 (1999): 764–91.

18. L. M. Roberts, G. M. Spreitzer, J. E. Dutton, R. Quinn, E. Heaphy, and B. Barker, "How to Play to Your Strengths," *Harvard Business Review* 83, no. 1 (2005): 74–80.

19. L. M. Roberts, J. E. Dutton, G. M. Spreitzer, E. Heaphy, and R. Quinn, "Composing the Reflected Best-Self Portrait: Building Pathways for Becoming Extraordinary in Work Organizations," *Academy of Management Review* 30 (2005): 712–36; G. M. Spreitzer, J. P. Stephens, and D. Sweetman, "The Reflected Best Self Field Experiment with Adolescent Leaders: Exploring the Psychological Resources Associated with Feedback Source and Valence," *Journal of Positive Psychology* 4 (2009): 331–48.

20. J. C. Maxwell, *Developing the Leaders around You* (Nashville, TN: Thomas Nelson, 1995).

21. M. Heinz, "Terrifying Moments with School Gunman Unfold in 911 Recording," CNN news service, August 22, 2013.

22. For the full transcript of the 911 call, see CNN news service, August 22, 2013, http://www.cnn.com/2013/08/22/us/georgia-school-shooting-911 -highlights/index.html.

6. Engage in Job Crafting

1. A. Wrzesniewski and J. E. Dutton, "Crafting a Job: Revisioning Employees as Active Crafters of their Work," *Academy of Management Review* 26 (2001): 179–201.

2. A. Wrzesniewski, J. M. Berg, and J. E. Dutton, "Turn the Job You Have into the Job You Want," *Harvard Business Review* (June 2010): 114–17.

3. A. M. Grant, *Give and Take: A Revolutionary Approach to Success* (New York: Viking, 2013).

4. J. M. Berg, A. Wrzesniewski, and J. E. Dutton, "Perceiving and Responding to Challenges in Job Crafting at Different Ranks: When Proactivity Requires Adaptivity," *Journal of Organizational Behavior* 31 (2010): 158–86.

5. A. Wrzesniewski and J. E. Dutton, "Crafting a Job: Revisioning Employees as Active Crafters of Their Work," *Academy of Management Review* 26 (2001): 179–201.

6. A. M. Grant and S. J. Ashford, "The Dynamics of Proactivity at Work," *Research in Organizational Behavior* 28 (2008): 3–34.

7. M. Tims, A. B. Bakker, and D. Derks, "Development and Validation of the Job Crafting Scale," *Journal of Vocational Behavior* 80 (2012): 173–86.

8. C. R. Leana, E. Appelbaum, and I. Shevchuk, "Work Process and Quality of Care in Early Childhood Education: The Role of Job Crafting," *Academy of Management Journal* 52, no. 6 (2009): 1169–92; A. Wrzesniewski, J. M. Berg, A. M. Grant, J. Kurkoski, and B. Welle, "Job Mindsets: Achieving Sustainable Gains in Expressed Happiness and Performance" (working paper, 2013); Tims, Bakker, and Derks, "Development and Validation of the Job Crafting Scale."

9. Tims, Bakker, and Derks, "Development and Validation of the Job Crafting Scale," 173–86. See also B. E. Ghitulescu, "Shaping Tasks and Relationships at Work: Examining the Antecedents and Consequences of Employee Job Crafting" (PhD diss., University of Pittsburgh, 2006).

10. Wrzesniewski et al., "Job Mindsets."

11. I. Ko, "Crafting a Job: Creating Optimal Experiences at Work" (PhD diss., Claremeont Graduate University, 2012).

12. J. M. Berg, A. M. Grant, and V. Johnson, "When Callings Are Calling: Crafting Work and Leisure in Pursuit of Unanswered Occupational Call-

ings," *Organization Science* 21 (2010): 973–94; see also G. R. Slemp, "Rethinking Work: Job Crafting, Self-Determination, and Employee Well-Being" (PhD diss., Monash University, Australia, 2013).

13. Wrzesniewski et al., "Job Mindsets."

14. Berg, Grant, and Johnson, "When Callings Are Calling."

15. A. Wrzesniewski, N. LoBuglio, J. E. Dutton, and J. M. Berg, "Job Crafting and Cultivating Positive Meaning and Identity in Work," in A. Bakker, ed., *Advances in Positive Organizational Psychology* (London: Emerald, 2013).

16. B. D. Rosso, K. H. Dekas, and A. Wrzesniewski, "On the Meaning of Work: A Theoretical Integration and Review," *Research in Organizational Behavior* 30 (2010): 91–127.

17. Ibid.

18. J. M. Lilius, "Recovery at Work: Understanding the Restorative Side of 'Depleting' Client Interactions," *Academy of Management Review* 37 (2012): 569–88.

19. A. Wrzesniewski et al., "Job Crafting and Cultivating Positive Meaning and Identity in Work."

20. Wrzesniewski et al., "Job Mindsets."

21. G. Spreitzer, K. Sutcliffe, J. E. Dutton, S. Sonenshein, and A. M. Grant, "A Socially Embedded Model of Thriving at Work," *Organization Science* 16 (2005): 537–49.

22. R. A. Eisenstat, "Managing Xerox's Multinational Development Center," Harvard Business School Teaching Note 490-029, March 1993.

23. C. Leana, E. Appelbaum, and I. Shevchuk, "Work Process and Quality of Care in Early Childhood Education: The Role of Job Crafting," *Academy of Management Journal* 52 (2009): 1169–92.

24. Wrzesniewski et al., "Job Mindsets"; see also Ghitulescu, "Shaping Tasks and Relationships at Work"; Slemp, "Rethinking Work."

25. J. E. Dutton and J. M. Berg, "Job Crafting at Burt's Bees," GlobaLens Case 1-428-854, November 2009.

7. Activate Virtuousness

1. A variety of studies confirm these relationships: e.g., L. M. Andersson, R. A. Giacalone, and C. L. Jurkiewicz, "On the Relationship of Hope and Gratitude to Corporate Social Responsibility," *Journal of Business Ethics* 70 (2007): 401–9; K. S. Cameron and A. Caza, "Organizational and Leadership Virtues and the Role of Forgiveness," *Journal of Leadership and Organizational Studies* 9 (2002): 33–48; J. E. Dutton, M. C. Worline, P. J. Frost, and J. Lilius, "Explaining Compassion Organizing," *Administrative Science Quarterly* 51,

no. 1 (2006): 59–96; C. Peterson and M. E. P. Seligman, *Character Strengths and Virtues* (New York: Oxford University Press, 2004); M. E. P. Seligman, *Authentic Happiness* (New York: Free Press, 2002); C. R. Snyder, *The Psychology of Hope* (New York: Free Press, 1994).

2. Examples of this research include T. Sherot, A. M. Riccardi, C. M. Raoi, and E. A. Phelps, "Neural Mechanisms Mediating Optimism Bias," *Nature* 450 (2007): 102–5; A. L. Hansen, B. H. Johnsen, J. F. Thayer, "Vagal Influence in the Regulation of Attention and Working Memory," *International Journal of Psychophysiology* 48 (2003): 263–74; B. E. Kok and B. L. Fredrickson, "Upward Spirals of the Heart: Autonomic Flexibility, as Indexed by Vagal Tone, Reciprocally and Prospectively Predicts Positive Emotions and Social Connectedness," *Biological Psychology* 85 (2010): 432–36.

3. Examples of influential writers who make this case are G. F. Davis, "The Rise and Fall of Finance and the End of the Society of Organizations," *Academy of Management Perspectives* 23 (2008): 27–44; M. C. Jenson, "Value Maximization, Stakeholder Theory and the Corporate Objective Function," *Business Ethics Quarterly* 12 (2002): 235–56.

4. Among the studies reporting these results are K. S. Cameron, C. E. Mora, T. Leutscher, and M. Calarco, "Effects of Positive Practices on Organizational Effectiveness," *Journal of Applied Behavioral Science* 47 (2011): 1–43; K. S. Cameron, D. Bright, and A. Caza, "Exploring the Relationships between Organizational Virtuousness and Performance," *American Behavioral Scientist* 4 (2004): 766–90; D. S. Bright, K. S. Cameron, and A. Caza, "The Amplifying and Buffering Effects of Virtuousness in Downsized Organizations," *Journal of Business Ethics* 64 (2006): 249–69.

5. A great deal of research on downsizing identifies its dysfunctional consequences; e.g., K. S. Cameron, "Strategic Organizational Downsizing: An Extreme Case," *Research in Organizational Behavior* 20 (1998): 185–229; K. S. Cameron, "Strategies for Successful Organizational Downsizing," *Human Resource Management Journal* 33 (1994): 89–112.

6. Cameron et al., "Effects of Positive Practices on Organizational Effectiveness."

7. The effects of individual virtues were not as predictive as virtuousness in the aggregate. This finding makes sense because rarely does one virtue exist in isolation and independent of other virtuous behaviors.

8. J. H. Gittell, K. S. Cameron, S. Lim, and V. Rivas, "Relationships, Layoffs, and Organizational Resilience," *Journal of Applied Behavioral Science* 42 (2006): 300–328; Cameron et al., "Effects of Positive Practices on Organizational Effectiveness."

9. The best studies on the effects of gratitude have been conducted by R. A. Emmons, "Acts of Gratitude in Organizations," in K. S. Cameron,

J. E. Dutton, and R. E. Quinn, eds., *Positive Organizational Scholarship*, 81–93 (San Francisco: Berrett-Koehler, 2003).

10. Cameron et al., "Effects of Positive Practices on Organizational Effectiveness."

11. B. L. Fredrickson, *Love 2.0* (New York: Hudson Street Press, 2013); R. Emmons, *Thanks!* (Boston: Houghton Mifflin, 2007).

12. See esp. Cameron and Caza, "Virtues and the Role of Forgiveness"; Bright, Cameron, and Caza, "Effects of Virtuousness in Downsized Organizations."

13. D. S. Bright and J. J. Exline, "Forgiveness at Four Levels: Intrapersonal, Relational, Organizational, and Collect-Group," in K. S. Cameron and G. M. Spreitzer, eds., *Oxford Handbook of Positive Organizational Scholarship*, 244–59 (New York: Oxford University Press, 2012).

14. See R. D. Hackett and G. Wang, "Virtues and Leadership: An Integrating Conceptual Framework Founded in Aristotelian and Confucian Perspectives on Virtues," *Management Decision* 50 (2012): 868–99.

15. An excellent discussion is found in T. M. Thrash and A. J. Elliot, "Inspiration as a Psychological Construct," *Journal of Personality and Social Psychology* 84 (2003): 871–89. Also see C. Peterson and M. E. P. Seligman, *Character Strengths and Virtues* (New York: Oxford University Press, 2004).

16. The best work on callings is A. Wrzesniewski, "Finding Positive Meaning in Work," in K. S. Cameron, J. E. Dutton, and R. E. Quinn, eds., *Positive Organizational Scholarship*, 296–308 (San Francisco: Berrett-Koehler, 2003). Also, A. Wrzesniewski, C. R. McCauley, P. Rozin, and B. Schwartz, "Jobs, Careers, and Callings: People's Relations to Their Work," *Journal of Research in Personality* 31 (1997): 21–33.

17. See, e.g., J. Haidt, "Elevation and the Positive Psychology of Morality," in C. L. M. Keyes and J. Haidt, eds., *Flourishing: Positive Psychology and the Life Well-Lived* (Cincinnati: Values in Action Institute, 2003); F. Andrews and S. Withey, *Social Indicators of Well-Being* (New York: Plenum, 1976); R. A. Emmons and J. A. Tsang, "The Grateful Disposition: A Conceptual and Empirical Topography," *Journal of Personality and Social Psychology* 82 (2002): 112–27.

18. See, e.g., S. B. Algoe and J. Haidt, "Witnessing Excellence in Action: The 'Other Praising' Emotions of Elevation, Gratitude, and Admiration," *Journal of Positive Psychology* 4 (2009): 105–27; N. M. Ashkanasy and C. E. Ashton-James, "Positive Emotions in Organizations: A Multilevel Framework," in D. L. Nelson and C. L. Cooper, eds., *Positive Organizational Behavior*, 57–73 (London: Sage, 2007); J. Haidt, *The Happiness Hypothesis: Finding Modern Truth in Ancient Wisdom* (New York: Basic Books, 2006).

19. For a summary, see K. S. Cameron, *Practicing Positive Leadership* (San Francisco: Berrett-Koehler, 2013). For a review of the effects of goal setting

on performance, see E. A. Locke and G. P. Latham, "Building a Practically Useful Theory of Goal Setting and Task Motivation: A 35-Year Odyssey," *American Psychologist* 57, no. 9 (2002): 705–17.

20. This argument is clearly delineated in Aristotle, *The Nicomachean Ethics*, Oxford World Classics (London: Oxford University Press, 2009).

8. Lead an Ethical Organization

1. D. E. Warren, "Constructive and Destructive Deviance in Organizations," *Academy of Management Review* 28 (2003): 622–32.

2. M. E. Brown, L. K. Treviño, and D. A. Harrison, "Ethical Leadership: A Social Learning Perspective for Construct Development and Testing," *Organizational Behavior and Human Decision Processes* 97 (2005): 117–34.

3. D. M. Mayer, K. Aquino, R. S. Greenbaum, and M. Kuenzi, "Who Displays Ethical Leadership and Why Does It Matter? An Examination of Antecedents and Consequences of Ethical Leadership," *Academy of Management Journal* 55 (2012): 151–71.

4. L. K. Treviño, M. Brown, and L. P. Hartman, "A Qualitative Investigation of Perceived Executive Ethical Leadership: Perceptions from Inside and Outside the Executive Suite," *Human Relations* 56 (2003): 5–37.

5. M. E. Brown and L. K. Treviño, "Ethical Leadership: A Review and Future Directions," *Leadership Quarterly* 17 (2006): 595–616.

6. L. K. Treviño and M. E. Brown, "Ethical Leadership," *The Oxford Handbook of Leadership and Organizations* (New York: Oxford University Press, forthcoming).

7. M. J. Neubert, D. S. Carlson, K. M. Kacmar, J. A. Roberts, and L. B. Chonko, "The Virtuous Influence of Ethical Leadership Behavior: Evidence from the Field," *Journal of Business Ethics* 90 (2009): 157–70.

8. P. Ruiz, C. Ruiz, and R. Martinez, "Improving the 'Leader-Follower' Relationship: Top Manager or Supervisor? The Ethical Leadership Trickle-Down Effect on Follower Job Response," *Journal of Business Ethics* 99 (2011): 587–608.

9. R. F. Piccolo, R. Greenbaum, D. H. Den Hartog, and R. Folger, "The Relationship between Ethical Leadership and Core Job Characteristics," *Journal of Organizational Behavior* 31 (2010): 259–78.

10. D. M. Mayer, M. Kuenzi, R. Greenbaum, M. Bardes, and R. Salvador, "How Low Does Ethical Leadership Flow? Test of a Trickle-Down Model," *Organizational Behavior and Human Decision Processes* 108 (2009): 1–13.

11. D. M. Mayer, M. Kuenzi, and R. L. Greenbaum, "Examining the Link between Ethical Leadership and Employee Misconduct: The Mediating Role of Ethical Climate," *Journal of Business Ethics* 95 (2010): 7–16.

12. F. O. Walumbwa, D. M. Mayer, P. Wang, H. Wang, K. Workman, and A. L. Christensen, "Linking Ethical Leadership to Employee Performance: The Roles of Leader-Member Exchange, Self-Efficacy, and Organizational Identification," *Organizational Behavior and Human Decision Processes* 115 (2011): 204–13.

13. A. W. Gouldner, "The Norm of Reciprocity: A Preliminary Statement," *American Sociological Review* 25 (1960): 161–78.

14. H. Tajfel, *Human Groups and Social Categories: Studies in Social Psychology* (New York: Cambridge University Press, 1981).

15. A. Bandura, *Social Learning Theory* (Englewood Cliffs, NJ: Prentice-Hall, 1977).

16. A. Bandura, *Social Foundations of Thought and Action: A Social Cognitive Theory* (Englewood Cliffs, NJ: Prentice Hall, 1986).

17. T. Simons, "Behavioral Integrity: The Perceived Alignment between Managers' Words and Deeds as a Research Focus," *Organization Science* 13 (2002): 18–35.

18. L. K. Treviño and M. E. Brown, "Managing to Be Ethical: Debunking Five Business Ethics Myths," *Academy of Management Executive* 18 (2004): 69–81.

19. A. Bandura, "Moral Disengagement in the Perpetuation of Inhumanities," *Personality and Social Psychology Review* 3 (1999): 193–209.

20. L. K. Treviño, G. R. Weaver, and M. E. Brown, "It's Lovely at the Top: Hierarchical Levels, Identities, and Perceptions of Organizational Ethics," *Business Ethics Quarterly* 18 (2008): 233–52.

21. L. K. Treviño and K. A. Nelson, *Managing Business Ethics: Straight Talk about How to Do It Right*, 5th ed. (Hoboken, NJ: Wiley, 2011).

22. B. Schneider, "The People Make the Place," *Personnel Psychology* 40 (1987): 437–53.

23. A. Wrzesniewski, J. E. Dutton, and G. Debebe, "Interpersonal Sense-Making and the Meaning of Work," *Research in Organizational Behavior* 25 (2003): 93–135.

9. Imbue the Organization with a Higher Purpose

1. B. Holmstrom, "Moral Hazard and Observability," *Bell Journal of Economics* 10, no. 1 (Spring 1979): 74–91.

2. A. V. Thakor and R. E. Quinn, "The Economics of Higher Purpose" (working paper, St. Louis: Washington University, February 2013). (Available from the authors.)

3. M. F. Steger, "Meaning in Life," in S. J. Lopez and C. R. Snyder, eds., *Oxford Handbook of Positive Psychology*, 679–87 (New York: Oxford University Press, 2009).

4. J. M. Burns, *Leadership* (New York: Harper & Row, 1978).

5. B. M. Bass, *Leadership and Performance beyond Expectations* (New York: Harper & Row, 1985).

6. B. J. Hoffman, B. H. Bynum, R. F. Piccolo, and A. W. Sutton, "Person-Organization Value Convergence: How Transformational Leaders Influence Work Group Effectiveness," *Academy of Management Journal* 54, no. 1 (2011): 779–96.

7. B. M. Bass and B. J. Avolio, *MLQ Multifactor Leadership Questionnaire* (Redwood City, CA: Mind Garden, 1995).

8. G. M. Spreitzer, "Psychological Empowerment in the Workplace: Dimensions, Measurement and Validation," *Academy of Management Journal* 38, no. 5 (1995): 1442–65.

9. B. J. Avolio, J. Griffith, T. S. Wernsing, and F. O. Walumbwa, "What Is Authentic Leadership Development?" in P. A. Linley, S. Harrington, and N. Garcea, eds., *Oxford Handbook of Positive Psychology and Work*, 39–51 (New York: Oxford University Press, 2010).

10. K. E. Weick, "Positive Organizing and Organizational Tragedy," in K. S. Cameron, J. E. Dutton, and R. E. Quinn, eds., *Positive Organizational Scholarship: Foundations of a New Discipline*, 66–80 (San Francisco: Berrett-Koehler, 2003).

11. R. S. Sisodia, D. B. Wolf, and J. N. Shet, *Firms of Endearment: How World Class Companies Profit from Passion and Purpose* (Upper Saddle River, NJ: Wharton School, 2007).

12. P. B. Vaill, "The Purposing of High-Performing Systems," *Organizational Dynamics* 11 (Autumn 1982): 23–39.

13. R. W. Quinn and R. E. Quinn, *Lift: Becoming a Positive Force in Any Situation* (San Francisco, CA: Berrett-Koehler, 2009).

14. G. Yukl, *Leadership in Organizations: Global Edition* (Boston: Pearson, 2013).

15. Ibid.

16. Ibid.

17. Ibid., p. 103.

18. Ibid., p. 109.

10. Cultivate Hope

1. http://www.nobelprize.org/nobel_prizes/peace/laureates.

2. B. Obama, The Ebenezer Baptist Church Address, 20 January 2008, Atlanta.

3. N. Mandela, *Long Walk to Freedom: The Autobiography of Nelson Mandela* (New York: Back Bay Books, 1995); K. Spink, *Mother Theresa: A Complete*

Authorized Biography (New York: HarperCollins, 1998); D. Tutu and M. Tutu, *Made for Goodness: And Why This Makes All the Difference* (New York: HarperOne, 2011); R. Branson, *Screw Business as Usual* (New York: Portfolio/ Penguin, 2011); M. Yunus, *Creating a World without Poverty: Social Business and the Future of Capitalism* (New York: PublicAffairs, 2007).

4. A. Razeghi, *Hope: How Triumphant Leaders Create the Future* (San Francisco: Jossey-Bass, 2006), 35, 63.

5. C. J. Farran, K. A. Herth, J. M. Popovich, *Hope and Hopelessness, Critical Clinical Constructs* (Thousand Oaks, CA: Sage, 1995).

6. O. Branzei, "Social Change Agentry Work: Understanding the Hopeful (Re)Production of Social Change," in K. Golden-Biddle and J. E. Dutton, eds., *Exploring Positive Social Change and Organizations: Building a Theoretical and Research Foundation* (New York: Routledge, 2012).

7. A. Carlsen and T. Pitsis, "Experiencing Hope in Organizational Lives," in L. M. Robert and J. E. Dutton, eds., *Exploring Positive Identities and Organizations: Building a Theoretical and Research Foundation*, 77–98 (New York: Psychology Press, 2009); C. R. Snyder, *Handbook of Hope: Theory, Measures and Applications* (San Diego: Academic Press, 2000); W. F. Lynch, *Images of Hope: Imagination as Healer of the Hopeless* (Baltimore: Helicon, 1965).

8. J. Elkington and P. Hartigan, *The Power of Unreasonable People: How Social Entrepreneurs Create Markets That Change the World*, Leadership for the Common Good (Boston: Harvard Business Press, 2002); E. M. W. Tong, B. M. Fredrickson, W. Chang, and Z. X. Lim, "Re-examining Hope: The Roles of Agency Thinking," *Cognition and Emotion* 24, no. 7 (2010): 1207–15.

9. Arlington's Academy of Hope, http://aahuganda.org/about-us/our -story; Building New Hope, http://www.buildingnewhope.org/about.html; Hope Worldwide, https://www.hopeww.org/sslpage.aspx?pid=211; Habitat for Humanity, http://www.habitat.org.

10. C. R. Snyder, *The Psychology of Hope: You Can Get There from Here* (New York: Free Press, 1994); J. D. Ludema, T. B. Wilmot, S. Srivastva, "Organizational Hope: Reaffirming the Constructive Task of Social and Organizational Inquiry," *Human Relations* 50, no. 8 (1997): 1015–52; E. Jansen, *Teaching with Poverty in Mind: What Being Poor Does to Kids' Brains and What Schools Can Do about It* (Alexandria, VA: Association for Supervision and Curriculum Development, 2009); G. Llopis, "5 Ways Leaders Keep Hope Alive in Difficult Times," *Forbes*, August 19, 2013, http://www.forbes.com/sites/glennllopis /2013/08/19/5-ways-leaders-keep-hope-alive-in-difficult-times/2.

11. T. Stat, in Razeghi, *Hope*, 83.

12. M. Yunus, http://www.imdb.com/media/rm2753871104/tt1669566 ?ref_=tt_ov_i.

13. http://www.thechangeblog.com/how-to-make-a-difference.

14. http://hereandnow.wbur.org/2013/07/22/ahmed-kathrada-mandela.

15. http://www.mtholyoke.edu/~gardn20a/classweb/prison.html.

16. http://www.nobelprize.org/mediaplayer/index.php?id=1855.

17. http://www.ted.com/speakers/ray_anderson.html.

18. W. A. Kahn, "Caring for the Caregivers: Patterns of Organizational Caregiving," *Administrative Science Quarterly* 38, no. 4 (1993): 539–63.

19. http://www.kissingitbetter.co.uk; Hope for New York; Helping People Help People, http://hfny.org/hurricane.

20. http://bluemarbledreams.wordpress.com/our-projects/inzozi-nziza-rwanda.

21. http://www.soaringwords.org.

22. Ela Bhatt has received multiple awards, including India's 2011 Indira Ghandi Peace Prize; http://www.sewa.org/About_Us.asp; E. R. Bhatt, *We Are Poor but So Many: The Story of Self-Employed Women in India* (New York: Oxford University Press, 2006); O. Branzei and S. Mehrotra, *SEWA: Leading with Hope* (London, Ontario, Canada: Ivey Publishing, 2014).

23. http://www.freethechildren.com/about-us/our-story; http://www.metowe.com/about-us/our-story.

24. http://www.weday.com.

11. Create Micro-moves for Organizational Change

1. The term "micro-moves" builds on the phrases "moves that matter" in J. E. Dutton, S. Ashford, R. O'Neill, and K. Lawrence, "Moves That Matter: Issue Selling and Organizational Change," *Academy of Management Journal* 44, no. 4 (2001): 716–36; and "micro-processes," in T. Reay, K. Golden-Biddle, and K. GermAnn, "Legitimizing a New Role: Small Wins and Microprocesses of Change," *Academy of Management Journal* 49, no. 5 (2006): 977–88.

2. N. Wingfield, "Microsoft Overhauls, the Apple Way," *New York Times*, July 21, 2013.

3. See J. E. Dutton et al., "Moves That Matter"; K. Golden-Biddle, "How to Change an Organization without Blowing It Up," *Sloan Management Review* (Winter 2013): 35–41; K. Golden-Biddle and J. E. Dutton, eds., *Using a Positive Lens to Explore Social Change and Organizations: Building a Theoretical and Research Foundation* (New York: Routledge, 2012); K. Golden-Biddle and J. Mao, "What Makes an Organizational Change Process Positive?" in K. S. Cameron and G. M. Spreitzer, eds., *Handbook of Positive Organizational Scholarship* (New York: Oxford University Press, 2012); J. Howard-Grenville, K. Golden-Biddle, J. Irwin, and J. Mao, "Liminality as Cultural Process for Cultural Change," *Organization Science* 22, no. 2 (2011): 522–39; D. Meyerson, "Radical Change the Quiet Way," *Harvard Business Review* (October 2001): 92–100.

4. K. Golden-Biddle and K. Correia, "Hope as Generative Dynamic in Transformational Change: Creating and Sustaining 'Collaborative Care' in the ThedaCare Health System," in Golden-Biddle and Dutton, *Using a Positive Lens to Explore Social Change and Organizations,* 241–66.

5. M. S. Feldman and A. M. Khademian, "Empowerment and Cascading Vitality," in K. S. Cameron, J. E. Dutton, and R. E. Quinn, eds., *Positive Organizational Scholarship: Foundations in a New Discipline,* 343–58 (San Francisco: Berrett-Koehler, 2003).

6. Meyerson, "Radical Change the Quiet Way."

7. J. E. Dutton, S. Ashford, K. Lawrence, and K. Miner-Rubino, "Red Light, Green Light: Making Sense of the Organizational Context for Issue Selling," *Organization Science* 13, no. 4 (2002): 355–69; J. E. Dutton and S. Ashford, "Selling Issues to Top Management," *Academy of Management Review* 18, no. 3 (1993): 397–428; J. Howard-Grenville, "Developing Issue Selling Effectiveness Over Time: Issue Selling as Resourcing," *Organization Science* 18, no. 4 (2007): 560–77; S. Sonenshein, "Being a Positive Social Change Agent through Issue Selling," in Golden-Biddle and Dutton, *Using a Positive Lens to Explore Social Change and Organizations,* 49–69; S. Sonenshein, "Crafting Social Issues at Work," *Academy of Management Journal* 49, no. 6 (2006): 1158–72.

8. Sonenshein, "Being a Positive Social Change Agent."

9. Golden-Biddle, "Change an Organization without Blowing It Up."

10. C. Bielaszka-DuVernay, "Redesigning Acute Care Processes in Wisconsin," *Health Affairs* (March 2011): 422–25.

11. G. Hamel with B. Breen, "Building an Innovation Democracy," in *The Future of Management* (Boston: Harvard Business School Press, 2007), 86.

12. R. Champagne, "Gore at 50," *Delaware Today,* July 2008.

13. Ibid.

14. http://www.gore.com/en_xx/careers/whoweare/rightforyou/working-at-gore.html.

15. Hamel, "Building an Innovation Democracy."

16. C. C. Manz, F. Shipper, and G. L. Stewart, "Everyone a Team Leader: Shared Influence at W. L. Gore and Associates," *Organizational Dynamics* 38, no. 3 (2009): 239–44.

17. Champagne, "Gore at 50."

12. Treat Employees as Resources, Not Resisters

1. J. P. Kotter, "Leading Change: Why Transformation Efforts Fail," *Harvard Business Review* 73, no. 2 (1995): 11–16.

2. J. D. Ford, L. W. Ford, and A. D'Amelio, "Resistance to Change: The Rest of the Story," *Academy of Management Review* 33, no. 2 (2008): 362–77.

3. B. M. Staw, L. E. Sandelands, and J. E. Dutton, "Threat-Rigidity Effects in Organizational Behavior: A Multilevel Analysis," *Administrative Science Quarterly* 26, no. 4 (1981): 501–24.

4. J. D. Ford, L. W. Ford, and A. D'Amelio, "Resistance to Change: The Rest of the Story," *Academy of Management Review* 33, no. 2 (2008): 362–77.

5. M. S. Feldman, "Organizational Routines as a Source of Continuous Change," *Organization Science* 11, no. 6 (2000): 611–29.

6. E. J. Langer and A. I. Piper, "The Prevention of Mindlessness," *Journal of Personality and Social Psychology* 53, no. 2 (1987): 280–87.

7. T. Baker and R. E. Nelson, "Creating Something from Nothing: Resource Construction through Entrepreneurial Bricolage," *Administrative Science Quarterly* 50, no. 3 (2005): 329–66.

8. S. Sonenshein, "How Organizations Foster the Creative Use of Resources," *Academy of Management Journal* (2014), doi:10.5465/amj.2012.0048.

9. S. Sonenshein and U. Dholakia, "Explaining Employee Engagement with Strategic Change Implementation: A Meaning-Making Approach," *Organization Science* 23, no. 1 (2012): 1–23.

10. C. G. Davis, S. Nolen-Hoeksema, and J. Larson, "Making Sense of Loss and Benefiting from the Experience: Two Construals of Meaning," *Journal of Personality and Social Psychology* 75, no. 2 (1998): 561–74.

11. S. Sonenshein, K. DeCelles, and J. E. Dutton, "It's Not Easy Being Green: Self-Evaluations and Their Role in Explaining Support of Environmental Issues," *Academy of Management Journal* 57, no. 1 (2014).

12. J. P. Kotter, *Leading Change* (Boston: Harvard Business School Press, 1996).

13. D. Kahneman, J. L. Knetsch, and R. H. Thaler, "Anomalies: The Endowment Effect, Loss Aversion, and Status Quo Bias," *Journal of Economic Perspectives* 5, no. 1 (1991): 193–206.

14. D. Kahneman and A. Tversky, "Choices, Values and Frames," *American Psychologist* 39, no. 4 (1984): 341–50.

15. G. Affleck and H. Tennen, "Construing Benefits from Adversity: Adaptational Significance and Dispositional Underpinnings," *Journal of Personality* 64, no. 4 (1996): 899–922.

16. K. A. DeCelles, P. E. Tesluk, and F. S. Taxman, "A Field Investigation of Multilevel Cynicism toward Change," *Organization Science* 24, no. 1 (2013): 154–71.

13. Create Opportunity from Crisis

1. Institute for Crisis Management, *Annual ICM Crisis Report: News Coverage of Business Crises During 2012*, vol. 22, no. 1 (2013).

2. E. James and L. Wooten, "Orientations of Positive Leadership in Times of Crisis," in K. S. Cameron and G. M. Spreitzer, eds., *The Oxford Handbook of Positive Organizational Scholarship*, 882–894 (New York: Oxford University Press, 2012).

3. L. Wooten and K. Cameron, "Enablers of a Positive Strategy: Leadership & Culture," in P. A. Linley, S. Harrington, and N. Garcea, eds., *The Oxford Handbook of Positive Psychology and Work*, 53–66 (New York: Oxford University Press, 2010).

4. J. E. Dutton and M. Glynn, "Positive Organizational Scholarship," in J. Barling and C. L. Cooper, eds., *The Sage Handbook of Organizational Behavior*, 693–711 (Thousand Oaks, CA: Sage, 2008).

5. K. Cameron, "Organizational Virtuousness and Performance," in K. S. Cameron, J. E. Dutton, and R. E. Quinn, eds., *Positive Organizational Scholarship* (San Francisco: Berrett-Koehler, 2003).

6. K. Cameron and A. Caza, "Developing Strategies for Responsible Leadership," in J. P. Doh and S. Stumph, eds., *Handbook on Responsible Leadership and Governance in Global Business* (Cheltenham, UK: Edward Elgar, 2006).

7. L. Wooten and E. James, "Linking Crisis Management and Leadership Competencies: The Role of Human Resource Development," *Advances in Human Resource Management Development* 10, no. 3 (2008): 352–79.

8. Ibid.

9. A. Edmondson, "Psychological Safety and Learning Behavior in Work Teams," *Administrative Science Quarterly* 44, no. 2 (1999): 350–83.

10. E. James and L. Wooten, "Crisis Leadership: Why It Matters," *European Financial Review* (December 2011): 60–64.

11. J. Moats, T. J. Chermack, and L. M. Dooley, "Using Scenarios to Develop Crisis Managers: Applications of Scenario Planning and Scenario-Based Training," *Advances in Developing Human Resources* 10 (2008): 397–424.

12. G. M. Spreitzer and S. Sonenshein, "Positive Deviance and Extraordinary Organizing," in Cameron, Dutton, and Quinn, *Positive Organizational Scholarship*, 207–24.

13. J. B. Brockner and E. H. James, "Toward an Understanding of When Executives See Crisis as Opportunity," *Journal of Applied Behavioral Science* 44, no. 1 (2008): 94–115.

14. K. Parson, "Ford Motor Company: A Lesson in Positive Crisis Leadership" (2013). This case was prepared by Ross School of Business Research Assistant Kelle Parson under the supervision of Professor Lynn Wooten.

15. YouGov BrandIndex, http://www.brandindex.com/ranking/us/2013 -mid/top-buzz-rankings.

Epilogue and Looking Forward

1. Idea of opening up new lines of sight inspired by K. Golden-Biddle, "Blink and You (Dis)miss Them: Coming to See New Lines of Sight," in A. Carlsen and J. E. Dutton, eds., *Research Alive: Exploring Generative Moments in Doing Qualitative Research*, 178–81 (Copenhagen: Copenhagen Business School Press, 2011).

Acknowledgments

This book has been a labor of love for the last eighteen months. We feel fortunate to work with such an impressive set of coauthors—some of the most respected thought leaders in positive organizational scholarship. We asked them to join us in fleshing out the best ideas on positive leadership—a sort of "greatest hits." The contributors to this volume have been wonderful to work with, even as we shortened the deadline for final chapters so that the book could be ready at an earlier date.

We thank the staff and the faculty of the Center for Positive Organizations (especially Managing Director Chris White) for their support on this book project. They read early drafts of chapters and encouraged us every step of the way. They are living out positive leadership each day in their roles. We also thank the leadership of the Ross School of Business at the University of Michigan, especially Dean Alison Davis-Blake, for making positive leadership a central part of the mission of our school.

We appreciate the organizational help of Lindsay Chmielewski for helping us herd all of our contributors as well as ourselves. We thank Joanne Gerstner, who helped us "harmonize" the chapters so that they had a common look and feel. We learned much about writing effectively from her. We also thank the editorial team at Berrett-Koehler, who inspired and supported us each step of the way. Neal Mallet helped us see the power in writing a book aimed at helping leaders rather than a book about teaching positive leadership. Thank you!

Last but not least, we thank our families for their understanding and love as we pushed through deadlines. We especially thank our husbands Lloyd Sandelands and Robert Schoeni for always being there to listen and to encourage.

On a final note, we appreciated working with each other. We learned so much as we challenged each other to think bigger and better.

JANE E. DUTTON AND
GRETCHEN M. SPREITZER

Ann Arbor, Michigan
January 9, 2014

Index

About the Authors

Oana Branzei is Associate Professor of Strategy at the Richard Ivey School of Business, Western University, and Visiting Professor at the Center for Positive Organizations and the Erb Institute for Global Sustainable Enterprise at the Ross School of Business, University of Michigan. Oana holds a doctorate from the Sauder School of Business, University of British Columbia, and an MBA from the University of Nebraska. Her academic projects explore the prosocial functions and positive impact of business, from social enterprises and social change initiatives to cross-sector innovation and community ecosystems. Her first edited book, *Dialogue in Critical Management Studies*, was published 2011.

Kim Cameron is the William Russell Kelly Professor of Management and Organizations in the Ross School of Business and Professor of Higher Education in the School of Education at the University of Michigan. He received BS and MS degrees from Brigham Young University and MA and PhD degrees from Yale University. His research on organizational virtuousness and other topics has been published in more than 130 scholarly articles and fifteen academic books. He was recently recognized as one of the top ten scholars in the organizational sciences whose work has been most frequently downloaded from Google.

Jane E. Dutton is the Robert L. Kahn Distinguished University Professor of Business Administration and Psychology at the Ross School of Business at the University of Michigan. She received her PhD from the Kellogg School of Management at Northwestern University. Jane's current research focuses on how the quality of connections between people at work links to individual and organizational flourishing. Her research explores compassion and organizations, the power of positive identities, as well as energy and organizations. Her previous work was on the management of strategic change. She is a cofounder of the Center for Positive Organizations.

Karen Golden-Biddle is the Questrom Professor in Management and Professor of Organizational Behavior at Boston University School of Management. She currently serves as Senior Associate Dean for Faculty and Research. Karen received her BA from Denison University and her MBA and PhD degrees from Case Western Reserve University. Her research and educational interests focus on organizational and system transformation with a special focus on understanding people's collective efforts for change that tap into frontline experience, engage discovery to imagine desired possibilities, and foster human agency in bringing about real and desired change.

Adam M. Grant is Professor of Management and the Class of 1965 Chair at Wharton business school and the author of *Give and Take* (2013), a *New York Times* and *Wall Street Journal* best-selling book that has been translated into more than two dozen languages. He received his BA from Harvard University and his PhD from the University of Michigan. He has been recognized as Wharton's top-rated teacher, one of *BusinessWeek*'s favorite professors, one of the world's top forty business professors under forty, and one of Malcolm Gladwell's favorite social science writers. He was profiled in the *New York Times* magazine cover story, "Is Giving the Secret to Getting Ahead?"

Erika Hayes James is the Senior Associate Dean for Executive Education and Professor of Business Administration at the Darden Graduate School of Business, University of Virginia. She conducts research in two primary areas: crisis leadership and workplace diversity, with an emphasis on women in leadership. Her research appears in numerous academic journals and popular press outlets. Professor James joined the Darden faculty in 2001. Before her Darden appointment, she served on the faculty at the Freeman School of Business at Tulane University and the Goizuetta Business School at Emory University, and was a visiting faculty member at the Harvard Business School.

Shirli Kopelman is a leading researcher, expert, and educator in the field of negotiations at the University of Michigan's Ross School of Business. Kopelman is also Faculty Director of Business Practice at the Center for Positive Organizations and Executive Director of the International Association for Conflict Management. Her research focuses on a positive process of mindful and strategic alignment of emotions, and its power to transform social exchange beyond an instrumental negotiation task to cocreation and generation of extraordinary success and well-being. Kopelman received awards for her cutting-edge negotiation research and for her outstanding achievements in the classroom.

Ramaswami Mahalingam is a cultural psychologist teaching at the University of Michigan, Ann Arbor, in the Personality and Social Contexts program. He is also affiliated with Women's Studies and Organizational Studies programs. His research focuses on mindfulness, leadership, and creativity. His current research examines the role of mobile technology in cultivating mindfulness. He has developed the mobile app Mindfulness Manager. Using the app, he is conducting an intervention study in a variety of organizational contexts. Integrating research on mindfulness and intersectionality, he has been investigating the relationship between critical intersectional awareness and mindfulness. He teaches an undergraduate course on mindfulness.

David M. Mayer is Assistant Professor of Management and Organizations at the University of Michigan's Stephen M. Ross School of Business. He conducts research, teaches, and consults in the areas of leadership and ethics. His research focuses on how leaders help create an environment that can discourage unethical behavior and promote helpful behavior. Drawing on this research, Dave works with individuals and organizations to improve their ability to lead ethically and to help improve the interpersonal dynamics of their employees. His research has been published in the top scholarly journals focusing on leadership and ethics, such as the *Academy of Management Journal, Journal of Applied Psychology, Organizational Behavior and Human Decision Processes*, and *Personnel Psychology*, and he is currently an associate editor of the *Academy of Management Journal*. He has worked with a variety of companies on these issues, such as the Ethics Resource Center, Giant Eagle, Humana, Lockheed Martin, Personnel Decisions Research Institute, P.H.I. Consulting Group, Schwan's, and SunTrust.

Christine Porath is Associate Professor at Georgetown University's McDonough School of Business. Porath received her PhD from the University of North Carolina at Chapel Hill's Kenan-Flagler Business School and taught for nine years at the University of Southern California's Marshall School of Business. Her research focuses on leadership, organizational culture, and change. She focuses not only on the effects of bad behavior, but also how organizations can create a more positive environment where people can thrive. Christine is coauthor of the book *The Cost of Bad Behavior*. Much of her recent work focuses on the benefits of civility and thriving.

Robert E. Quinn holds the Margaret Elliot Tracey Collegiate Professorship at the University of Michigan and serves on the faculty of Organization and Management at the Ross Business School. He is one of the cofounders and the current faculty codirector of the Center for Positive Organizations. Bob's research and teaching interests focus on leadership, organizational change, and effectiveness. He has published sixteen books on these subjects. He is particularly known for his work on the competing values framework. He has thirty years of experience consulting with major corporations and government agencies.

Gretchen M. Spreitzer is the Keith E. and Valerie J. Alessi Professor of Business Administration at the Ross School of Business at the University of Michigan. She is the codirector of the Center for Positive Organizations. Her research focuses on employee empowerment and leadership development, particularly within a context of organizational change and decline. Her most recent research is examining how organizations can enable thriving and enable employees' full potential. She has been elected to leadership positions in the Academy of Management and the Western Academy of Management.

Laura Morgan Roberts is an author, a professor, a researcher, a leadership development coach, and an organizational consultant. She is Professor of Psychology, Culture, and Organization Studies in Antioch University's PhD program in Leadership and Change. She is also a core faculty affiliate of the Center for Positive Organizations. A thought leader in the areas of authenticity, identity, diversity, strengths, and value creation, Laura coedited *Exploring Positive Identities and Organizations* with Jane M. Dutton. Laura earned her MA and PhD (Organizational Psychology) from the University of Michigan and BA (Psychology) from University of Virginia.

Scott Sonenshein is Associate Professor of Management at the Jones Graduate School of Business at Rice University, where he teaches courses in change and leadership. His studies examine the resourceful actions of employees to advance organizational and social/ethical change. He has conducted research in settings ranging from fashion to food trucks, banks to booksellers, and entrepreneurs to environmentalists. This work illuminates the skill, agency, and motivation of individuals to contribute to change and the corresponding organizational practices that foster these outcomes. He currently serves as an associate editor at the *Academy of Management Journal*.

Anjan V. Thakor is the John E. Simon Professor of Finance, Director of the PhD program, and Director of the WFA Center for Finance and Accounting Research at the Olin Business School, Washington University, in St. Louis. He holds a PhD from Northwestern University. His previous university faculty appointments include Michigan, Indiana, Northwestern, and UCLA. His areas of research, teaching, and consulting interest are asymmetric information, corporate finance, banking, and economics of higher purpose. He has published research articles in leading economics and finance journals, and in 2008, he was recognized as the fourth most prolific researcher globally in finance over the past fifty years.

Lynn Perry Wooten is Associate Dean of Undergraduate Programs at the Ross School of Business, University of Michigan. In this role, she is responsible for developing and implementing transformational educational experiences for Ross undergraduate students inside and outside of the classroom. She teaches organizational behavior, nonprofit management, and strategic consulting courses. Professor Wooten conducts research in the areas of positive organizing routines, diversity management, crisis leadership through resilience and organizational learning, and educational and leadership development of undergraduate students. Her research appears in academic journals, monographs, and popular press outlets.

Amy Wrzesniewski is Associate Professor of Organizational Behavior at Yale University's School of Management. Professor Wrzesniewski earned a BA in Psychology from the University of Pennsylvania and an MA and PhD in Organizational Psychology from the University of Michigan. She has won the IBM Faculty Award for her research, in addition to awards for her undergraduate, graduate, and executive teaching. Her research focuses on how people make meaning of their work in challenging contexts (e.g., stigmatized occupations, virtual contexts, absence of work), and the experience of work as a job, career, or calling.

Kim S. Cameron, Jane E. Dutton, and Robert E. Quinn,
Editors

Positive Organizational Scholarship
Foundations of a New Discipline

Featuring contributions by internationally renowned scholars, *Positive Organizational Scholarship* pioneered the exploration of the dynamics in organizations that lead to extraordinary individual and organizational performance. Just as positive psychology focuses on exploring optimal *individual* psychological states rather than pathological ones, *Positive Organizational Scholarship* focuses attention on optimal *organizational* states—the dynamics in organizations that lead to the development of human strength; foster resiliency in employees; make healing, restoration, and reconciliation possible; and cultivate extraordinary individual and organizational performance. Widely adopted as a university text, *Positive Organizational Scholarship* rigorously seeks to understand what represents the best of the human condition based on scholarly research and theory.

Hardcover, 480 pages, ISBN 978-1-57675-232-6
PDF ebook, ISBN 978-1-57675-966-0

Berrett–Koehler Publishers, Inc.
www.bkconnection.com

800.929.2929

Berrett–Koehler
Publishers

Berrett-Koehler is an independent publisher dedicated to an ambitious mission: *Creating a World That Works for All*.

We believe that to truly create a better world, action is needed at all levels—individual, organizational, and societal. At the individual level, our publications help people align their lives with their values and with their aspirations for a better world. At the organizational level, our publications promote progressive leadership and management practices, socially responsible approaches to business, and humane and effective organizations. At the societal level, our publications advance social and economic justice, shared prosperity, sustainability, and new solutions to national and global issues.

A major theme of our publications is "Opening Up New Space." Berrett-Koehler titles challenge conventional thinking, introduce new ideas, and foster positive change. Their common quest is changing the underlying beliefs, mindsets, institutions, and structures that keep generating the same cycles of problems, no matter who our leaders are or what improvement programs we adopt.

We strive to practice what we preach—to operate our publishing company in line with the ideas in our books. At the core of our approach is stewardship, which we define as a deep sense of responsibility to administer the company for the benefit of all of our "stakeholder" groups: authors, customers, employees, investors, service providers, and the communities and environment around us.

We are grateful to the thousands of readers, authors, and other friends of the company who consider themselves to be part of the "BK Community." We hope that you, too, will join us in our mission.

A BK Business Book

This book is part of our BK Business series. BK Business titles pioneer new and progressive leadership and management practices in all types of public, private, and nonprofit organizations. They promote socially responsible approaches to business, innovative organizational change methods, and more humane and effective organizations.

Berrett–Koehler
Publishers

A community dedicated to creating
a world that works for all

Dear Reader,

Thank you for picking up this book and joining our worldwide community of Berrett-Koehler readers. We share ideas that bring positive change into people's lives, organizations, and society.

To welcome you, we'd like to offer you a free e-book. You can pick from among twelve of our bestselling books by entering the promotional code BKP92E here: http://www.bkconnection.com/welcome.

When you claim your free e-book, we'll also send you a copy of our e-newsletter, the *BK Communiqué*. Although you're free to unsubscribe, there are many benefits to sticking around. In every issue of our newsletter you'll find

- A free e-book
- Tips from famous authors
- Discounts on spotlight titles
- Hilarious insider publishing news
- A chance to win a prize for answering a riddle

Best of all, our readers tell us, "Your newsletter is the only one I actually read." So claim your gift today, and please stay in touch!

Sincerely,

Charlotte Ashlock
Steward of the BK Website

Questions? Comments? Contact me at bkcommunity@bkpub.com.